CELEBRATING SERVICE

CELEBRATING SERVICE

John and Agnes Sturt

eagle

Guildford, Surrey

British Library Cataloguing in Publication Data. A catalogue record for this book is available from the British Library.

Published by Eagle Publishing Ltd, PO Box 530, Guildford, Surrey GU2 4FH.

Typeset by Eagle Publishing
Printed by Cox & Wyman
ISBN No: 0 86347 372 5

Dedicated to our parents,

Keith & Janet Broughton and Reginald & Marjory Sturt

who modelled a life of service for us.

Contents

Acknowledgements

We wish to freely acknowledge the help of many people who have been involved in the gestation and birth of this book. As we drew on the expertise and wisdom of friends, we became profoundly grateful for the amazing number of friends we have. Some of them are listed in the references, particularly in connection with Chapter Six, and many others have provided advice and encouragement. Our thanks to Sue Knox for help with the computer.

We are especially grateful to those who carefully critiqued parts or the whole of the manuscript: Rev John McAlpine, Dr John Hitchen, Rev Roger Elley-Brown, Richard Charmley, Margaret Corin, Elaine and Steve McFadzean, Dr Murray Harris, Neville Taylor, Dr Peter Lineham, Rev David Jenkins, Jenny Fountain, Chris Grantham, Dr Cathy Ross, Ken Tracey, Sue Wavre. This has resulted in numerous re-writes, but hopefully has produced an improved finished product.

Our long-suffering publisher has greatly encouraged us, and we are delighted to be published with Eagle again.

Foreword

Anybody trying to commend a concept of 'service' to today's post-modern men and women has an almost impossible task. Among the rich New Testament vocabulary, the two commonest word groups about service relate either to servants (originally some-body who waited at table), or to slaves. Waiters are seen to be slightly comic and have foreign accents like Basil Fawlty's incompetent employee from Barcelona, Manuel. Anybody working for Fawlty has our sympathy, but nobody would want his job. Slaves are thought of as black-skinned, a shameful episode in human history, of which we whites are all properly ashamed. The whole concept of being a servant is nauseating in these more enlightened and egalitarian days. That some are born to live upstairs and be waited on hand and foot by those who by an accident of birth live downstairs (not to mention unfortunate governesses who live halfway between) is an unpleasant memory from a bygone era. Even then it was under-stood that the Admirable Crichton was an immeasurably superior human being to his employers and we all respect Wodehouse's Jeeves, yet despise a creature like Bertie Wooster.

True, in Kazuo Ishiguro's *The Remains of the Day* the butler, Mr Stephens, seems a truly noble if tragic human being while his poor father is depicted as a rather pathetic figure. Yet 'his lordship' at Darlington Hall proves, with all his aristocratic acceptance of the service of others, to be a Nazi sympathiser and utterly unworthy of the respectful demeanour and sacrificial loyalty that his butler gives him in unquestioning,

9

faithful service. We shudder at such social arrangements today, shun all subservience and are glad that Lord Emsworth, Bertie Wooster and his cronies no longer determine our destinies in the House of Lords.

It is perhaps worth mentioning that this repugnance for being a slave and hatred of subservience and indebtedness, is nothing new. This feeling would have been shared by many of the first hearers of Jesus of Nazareth and those who subsequently listened to the teaching of Peter, Paul and others of his disciples. That Jesus himself voluntarily humbled himself and took the form of a slave, was a challenge to human pride then as much as it still is today.

Our underlying problem is that there are few, if any, heroes left in the modern world who command our respect. The dashing actors we first saw playing the imperturbable James Bond are now rather tatty, ageing old buffers. Detectives like Inspector Frost, Inspector Morse and Jane Tennyson have bumbling or corrupt superior officers for whom we lose all respect. In historical thrillers, our sympathies are all with Hornblower and Sharpe in their struggle against their incompetent superiors. We may have sports heroes – athletes, footballers and cricketers, then we discover they are cheating by taking drugs, or are actually fixing matches for money! Can we respect politicians? The question is almost laughably unnecessary: In the western democracies we suspect that our political leaders are ambitious and self-serving opportunists and in the rest of the world everybody knows they are.

Can we salvage then the concept of 'service' at all? Naval war films like *In Which We Serve* and films on Dunkirk or the Battle of Britain show that sacrificial service to the extent of laying down one's life for one's community is still admired, even if the 1914–18 War threw up generals willing to abandon their fellow men to needless slaughter. We still find the concept of 'serving' within family life, with mothers (and even fathers) determined to serve their children and slaving away to bring in enough income to keep them fed and clothed. The best, lasting marriages still go on revealing a determination to love and indeed to serve our dearest with all our energies to the very end of our lives. There also remains still a laudable desire on the part of younger people to serve our fellow human beings, especially those in need and poverty. This altruistic desire to help others without hidden motives of monetary gain or self-promotion which gives us hope that the wider-ranging concerns of this book may find a response in such readers.

Religious pluralism has led many to downgrade Jesus of Nazareth and put him on a level with other founders of world religions, as one of many options in the 'faith' supermarket. It is only when individuals realise that here at last we have a 'hero' truly worthy of our grateful service, that we shall understand what this book means by the concept of 'service'. For us to become servants of the Lord Jesus Christ all our days (indeed, to be his willing bond-slaves ready to put his cause and his kingdom before all other calls on our energies and loyalties), is to find at last a life worth living. Years ago Tom Howard, in rebellion against the Christian home in which he was brought up, wrote about his rediscovery of the authentic Jesus Christ of the Bible in a book called *Christ the Tiger*.

> We found him towering above us, scorching our efforts into clinkers, and recalling us to wildness and risk and humility and love . . . Try as we might, we could not own him. We could not incarcerate him. For he always emerged as our judge, exposing our cynicism and fright by the candour and boldness of his love. He tore our secularist schemes to ribbons by announcing doom and our religious schemes to tatters by announcing love.

11

We need to realise that here at last is someone utterly worthy of our respect, worship and willing service, the Prince of Life, who laid down his life for me and every other human being. He himself is more reliable, more consistently overflowing with goodness and mercy, than we could conceive in our wildest longings for goodness and perfection. Howard has this Christ, the image of the invisible God, addressing us in the following terms:

> Return, return and think again what I have asked of you: to follow justice, and love mercy, and do your job or work, and love one another, and give me the worship of your heart – your *heart* – and be merry and thankful and lowly, and not pompous and gaunt and sere.

The authentic Lord Jesus of the Bible is worthy of our service, and will teach us how to serve. This book will get you going in discovering this great adventure in serving.

Michael Griffiths
Guildford, May 2000

Prequel

Many readers skip the Introduction of a book, and you may wish to do that too. However, there is something we would like to say as a *prequel* so that the *sequel* might make more sense.

You may be wondering, 'Why write a book about service? Isn't it rather out of date and incompatible with modern thinking? Surely the purpose of life is to be fulfilled, discover your uniqueness and actualise your potential so you can get the most out of life? Happiness comes from doing your own thing, not serving someone else.' We hope to show that being a servant is in fact the way to meaning and fulfilment in life. Jesus said, 'I have come that they may have life, and have it to the full',[1] but he is also the one who taught us most about being a servant and who modelled this in his own life.

In our previous books we focused on discovering who we are and how to become the person God intends each one of us to be.[2] *Created for Love* examines the concept of self-esteem and healthy ways to grow in a sense of self-worth. Many people, including some Christians, have an inadequate view of themselves. To have a good self-esteem means primarily to see ourselves as God sees us and value ourselves as he does. When we love, value and esteem ourselves we can then forget about ourselves and serve others.

The second book, *Created for Intimacy*, deals with the problem of loneliness and how to develop intimate relationships with ourselves, others and God. This is something most people long for. The third title, *Created to be Whole*, looks at growth to wholeness and maturity: physically, mentally, emotionally, socially and spiritually. That book completes the trilogy, but the progression of ideas is incomplete. Although it's good to have a healthy self-esteem, intimate relationships and to be a whole person, who is it all for? Certainly it is not only for my benefit. The goal of personal growth and maturity is so that I might *become a better servant.* Hence we felt compelled to write this book, aiming to show how an attitude of service underlies healthy living. Service is at the heart of the Christian message.

Being a servant permeates all aspects of life and relation-ships. It is not something you do just when you feel like it, but service flows out of a servant attitude and world-view. The Scriptures are full of the concept of service and they assure us that the only way to true freedom is by becoming Christ's servant/slave. If this concept is too disturbing, you might be wise not to read any further.

While we base what we say in this book unashamedly on biblical values, we are not writing in a theoretical vacuum. The book is partly autobiographical, and we have also drawn on the opinions and life experiences of many others to illustrate the ideas. We interviewed more than fifty people about how they see the service aspects of their profession. At the end of each chapter there are a few reflections and exercises for personal application. These can be worked through on your own or, preferably, in a group setting. May we all learn how to follow Peter's advice, 'Live as free men, but do not use your freedom as a cover-up for evil. Live as servants [slaves] of God.'[3]

John and Agnes Sturt
211b St Andrews Rd,
Epsom, Auckland 1004,
New Zealand.
E-mail <johnsturt@compuserve.com>

Overview of this Book

Chapter One sets the stage by contrasting the Christian value system with that of the world in which we live: the conflict of either being other-focussed or self-focussed. Christian service is an expression of unconditional love, through serving Christ and serving others.

Chapter Two explores how the service principle affects the whole of our lifestyle. This can be expressed through friendship, hospitality, marriage, parenting, healing and prayer. The principle of service underlies every aspect of healthy living.

Chapter Three describes the biblical basis for service, which is a concept that runs right through Scripture. Jesus, the perfect servant and Servant King modelled service and calls us to be his servants. The apostles took this seriously, calling themselves 'slaves of Christ.' This is the way for us to follow.

Chapter Four addresses the challenge of being properly equipped for service. We have all been given natural and spiritual gifts that need to be developed. God has provided us with the resources and 'fuel' so that our service can be effective.

Chapter Five looks at the rewards of service. We do not serve God for a reward but because we love him. However, he is no one's debtor, and the rewards of service are rich and varied, both here on earth and in eternity.

Chapter Six Shows how Christians have a powerful motive for service, but not a monopoly on it, and there is a great interest in humanitarian service today. There are also many 'serving professions', such as medicine, nursing, teaching, social work, law and others. We explore these, as well as the many opportunities to serve within the church and in para-church organisations.

Chapter Seven This final chapter looks at cross-cultural mission service, starting with a brief history of Christian missions over the past two millennia. We look briefly at what is being done today and then address the challenge, call, cost and opportunities for cross-cultural mission service overseas and at home.

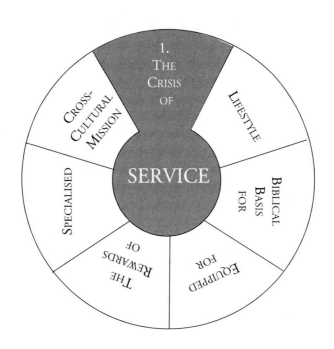

1.
THE
CRISIS
OF

LIFESTYLE

BIBLICAL
BASIS
FOR

EQUIPPED
FOR

THE
REWARDS
OF

SPECIALISED

CROSS-
CULTURAL
MISSION

SERVICE

One

The Crisis of Service

The purpose to life is not 'to have and to hold' but to 'give and to serve.' There can be no other meaning.
Sir Wilfred Grenfell, 1865–1940[1]

We all start life totally self-oriented, living in a world of one. This is only natural, because a baby regards itself as the centre of the universe. Psychologists assure us that in the first few months of life (known as the 'autistic period') an infant makes no distinction between itself and the rest of the world. The world is there for its own benefit and comfort, and the baby usually has only to cry or smile to have all needs met. The first major challenge in life is the discovery that there are other people in our world who also have needs. Socialisation is the process of adjusting in healthy ways to this challenge.

THE CRISIS

This conflict provides us with our first major crisis in life, which becomes increasingly difficult as we grow older. The challenge is between meeting our own needs and responding to those of others; between being *self-focused* or *other-focused*, and finding an appropriate balance between the two. We all grow up in a society which is primarily self-focused. The philosophy of most people is 'Look after Number One. I'll make sure that my needs are met before I think of others, if at all.' The contrast is between serving myself and serving others. But why describe it in terms of service?

We all serve someone or something. These 'gods' come in different forms, such as ambition, power, money, work, 'toys', pleasure, sex, sport, drugs, food and many others. 'A man is a slave to whatever controls him.'[2] The objects we serve may vary at the different stages of life, but most of them are ultimately ways of self-serving and meeting our own perceived needs.

This is where genuine Christianity is at variance with other philosophies, by stressing the importance of loving God with all your heart, soul and mind and loving your neighbour as you love yourself.[3] It is not easy to move from being *self-focused* to becoming *other-focused*. Our attempts to reach out to others are often tinged with mixed motives as we try to meet our own needs as well. However, genuine other-centredness is evidence of maturity and provides fulfilment. This becomes a crisis for the Christian who takes the value system of Jesus seriously, because he turns the world's philosophies upside down. It is a spiritual battle. Archbishop William Temple wrote, 'The only way to deliver me from my self-centredness is by winning my heart's devotion, the total allegiance of my will to God.'[4]

Mature people do not neglect their own physical, emotional and spiritual health but keep these in *balance* with their desire to reach out to others. In their relationships, they are able to shift the focus from themselves by setting aside their own desires and plans temporarily, or even permanently, in their concern for the welfare of others. As Paul expressed it: 'Each of you should look not only to your own interests, but also to the interests of others.'[5]

This is not easy to do.

GIVING AND RECEIVING

The paradox is that the more we serve and give to others, the more we are blessed ourselves. Jesus expressed it this way:

> Give and it shall be given to you. A good measure, pressed down, shaken together and running over, will be poured into your lap. For with the measure you use, it will be measured to you.[6]

Jesus is not telling us to give in order that we might receive, but that receiving is the natural consequence of giving. This is a principle of life. The farmer who 'sows generously will also reap generously'.[7] In business, the more money a person invests wisely, the greater is the return. Many people have discovered that the more they give away to others, the more they receive. Solomon stated this general principle three thousand years ago: 'It is possible to give away and become richer! It is also possible to hold on too tightly and lose everything. Yes, the liberal man shall be rich. By watering others, he waters himself.'[8] This principle can be summed up in a more modern proverb, 'You make a living by what you get; you make a life by what you give.'

This dynamic is especially true in relationships. The more we invest in people, the more we are likely to receive from them. However, if I go into a friendship or marriage thinking mainly about how much I can get out of it, the relationship will certainly suffer. If two people have a strong desire to give to one another, their relationship will grow in strength and intimacy. Even in situations where the giving may not be reciprocated, the one who gives will always be blessed through the giving.

Susan enjoyed her life at university. She was outgoing and soon made friends, becoming close to two girls in her year. One of them, Mary, was a bright student but rather insecure. She was very competitive and saw Susan as a threat academically as well as socially; she gained whatever she could from being with her but gave little back in return. They had quite a lot in common and Susan wanted to develop their friendship, but she always found herself slightly drained of energy after being with Mary.

Her other friend, Judy, was quite different. After spending time together, Susan felt relaxed and energised. They did not place demands on one another, and were genuinely interested in what was going on for the other person. They were able to share some of their struggles, become vulnerable to one another, encourage each other and develop a warm friendship. However, Susan persisted in her relationship with Mary and tried to include her as much as possible in her life. It was hard work, but by the end of the year Mary had started to open up and even showed concern for some of Susan's needs.

Another paradox in life is that we *keep what we give away*. Jesus implies this in his well-known 'Sermon on the Mount':

> 'Don't hoard treasure down here where it gets eaten by moths and corroded by rust – worse! – stolen by burglars. Stockpile treasure in heaven, where it is safe from moth and rust and burglars. It's obvious isn't it? The place where your treasure is, is the place where you will most want to be, and end up being.'[9]

How do we 'stockpile treasure in heaven'? By giving it away and using it for the blessing of others on earth. The world advises us: 'Don't hoard your money, spend it now because you can't take it with you.' Jesus is also saying in effect, 'Don't hoard your money, but you *can* take it with you if you give it away and invest your resources for the welfare of others.' Paul encouraged Christians to 'excel in this grace of giving'.[10]

There is a reciprocal aspect to this process of giving and receiving. We need to be able to *accept* the gifts, love and service of others as well as give to them. Some people find this difficult. They are embarrassed to receive a gift, or even a compliment, or to let others serve them in some way. This is often because they have a poor sense of self-worth and as a result are more worried about how they can repay the giver than enjoy the gift. In refusing to receive gifts or expressions of love and service from others, we are effectively denying them the pleasure and benefits of giving. By not receiving graciously we dishonour rather than bless the giver. Richard Gillard expressed this well in the first verse of the *Servant Song*:

Brother (sister), let me be your servant,
Let me be as Christ to you,
Pray that I might have the grace,
To let you be my servant too.[11]

UNCONDITIONAL LOVE

The main word for love in the New Testament is '*agapē*', which means '**gift-love**'. This differentiates it from all other types of human love, which are forms of '**need-love**', i.e. expressions of our need to be loved. C.S. Lewis explores this in his classic, *The Four Loves*.[12] He shows that *agapē* differs from the other forms of love defined in the Greek language: *eros* (erotic love), *storgë* (natural affection) and *philia* (friendship). Agape-love is unconditional love; the other aspects of love are primarily conditional responses.

Agape-love is not natural to us but can develop as a person matures. We learn it first as we receive unconditional love from others, and then as we come to know God's unconditional love. Most of the love that we experience in this world is *conditional.* As children, our parents often appear to love us only if we

23

behave, don't make too much noise, keep our rooms tidy, succeed at school or excel at sport. For some children the list is endless and love for them has to be earned, or that is how it appears to them. As adults, we are usually valued, affirmed and loved if we are successful, good looking, intelligent, well off, and do the politically correct thing. Again, love has to be earned.

Unconditional love is not just difficult, it is impossible through human effort alone. As parents, friends or lovers we all need God's love in our lives to give us the strength and perseverance to love others unconditionally, because this is essentially a divine form of loving. This is how God loves us.[13] His love is not dependent on our loving him first, or even in return. He loves us just as much whether we love him or reject him.

Unconditional love transforms us. John Powell expressed it this way: 'Unconditional love is liberating. It frees the loved one to be authentic and real. Conditional love leaves the loved one only the course of conformity.'[14] To be loved unconditionally is one of the deepest longings of every human being. If I am only loved conditionally, I am left with doubt as to my real worth, and a lurking fear that if I don't perform adequately that love may be withdrawn. The kind of love I receive has a major influence on the kind of person I become, and whether I have a strong or weak sense of self-worth. An awareness of the power of unconditional love in our own lives can stimulate us to offer this kind of loving to others.

To Serve is to Love

True service is ultimately an expression of love. Love is a transitive verb, so it requires an object. The love we feel inside does not really become love until it is given away in some act of kindness or service. Agape-love is more related to the will than

24

to the emotions. It is a decision more than a feeling, and to express love through service may not be the immediate response to feeling loving. Loving service usually follows a desire to serve rather than a desire to love. The feeling of love often follows the act of service rather than preceding it.

Brent was travelling home one dark and rainy night. It was cold and he felt jaded after a hectic day. He was running late and looked forward to getting home and having a good meal. As he rounded a corner, his headlights picked out a car parked by the side of the road and the figure of a woman bending over trying to change a wheel. Brent didn't have any desire to stop and help her, but he did anyway. The wheel nuts were tight and it required a lot of effort to shift them. By the time he had changed the tyre he was wet and his hands were dirty. He told me afterwards that when he stopped he had no warm feelings towards the stranded driver, but as he drove away he was aware of a sense of compassion and was pleased with what he had done. His action was prompted by a commitment to serve and this was followed by the feeling of love.

Loving service can be as much of a surprise to the giver as to the receiver. This is an example of 'your left hand not knowing what your right hand is doing'.[15] Love is unaware of itself. The service of love is a spontaneous expression from the heart rather than an act planned for its effect on others. An attitude of service can become a way of life and part of who we are. Once we have made the decision that this is how we want to live, with God's help, we can develop a 'servant heart'. This means we will be likely to choose the path of service when the opportunity presents without having to think too much about it. The choice to serve becomes less of a struggle and more an expression of our freedom. St Paul wrote: 'Do not use your freedom to indulge the sinful nature; rather, serve one another in love.'[16]

DIMENSIONS OF CHRISTIAN SERVICE

We can think of Christian service at several levels which overlap and impinge on each other.

Serving Christ

This is the foundation of service and also its goal.

Because we love Jesus and owe our lives and everything that we are to him, it follows that we will want to serve him, despite the fact that our bias is to serve ourselves. Of course, this dual motivation results in a constant battle within: to do what I really want to do and not end up doing the things I don't want to do.[17] Our Lord warned us: 'No-one can serve two masters. Either he will hate the one and love the other, or he will be devoted to the one and despise the other.'[18]

We need a strong love for Jesus and the power of the Holy Spirit in order to serve him effectively; but this can become the driving force in our lives, as it did for Paul, who said: 'Christ's love compels us.'[19] He described his three years in Ephesus in this way: 'I served the Lord with great humility and with tears.'[20] If we have this attitude of serving the Lord, it will colour all our service, however unpleasant that service may seem to be.

In the ancient world, the life of a slave was not a happy existence. When Paul wrote to Christian slaves in Ephesus, he did not condone the practice of slavery but pointed out to them that they were also slaves of Christ, as he was himself. So he encouraged them to 'Serve wholeheartedly, as if you were serving the Lord, not men'.[21] This attitude may not change our circumstances, but it will change us.

An Indian journalist once questioned Mother Theresa, 'Mother, tell me how you have trained yourself to touch people with loathsome diseases like leprosy and gangrene. Aren't you revolted by people filthy with dysentery, or cholera and vomit?'

THE CRISIS OF SERVICE

She looked him squarely in the eye and replied, 'I see Jesus in every human being. I say to myself, "This is hungry Jesus, I must feed him. This is sick Jesus, this one has gangrene, dysentery or cholera. I must wash him and tend to him. I serve them because I love Jesus." '[22]

Serving the Church

If we belong to the Lord, we are part of the Church, members of 'his body'. Being part of the Church is not an option for a Christian, it is implicit in being a disciple of Christ. We are called to be God's new community on earth. Paul Tournier once said, 'There are two things we cannot do alone, one is to be married and the other is to be a Christian.' Of recent years, more and more Christians have become disillusioned with the institutional Church, and often for valid reasons. We can all find some faults with our own church fellowship, because it is made up of imperfect human beings like ourselves.

However, the Church is God's new community on earth, and for Christians to disassociate themselves from it results in loss for both them and the Church.[23] All believers can find some significant avenue of service within the Church. (We touch on this again in Chapter Four.) Paul considered serving the Church to be a significant part of his calling: 'I have become its servant by the commission God gave me to present to you the word of God in its fulness.'[24]

Paul used several metaphors to describe the Church: a *field* where God's seed is planted and grows; a *building* to which all Christians contribute, brick by brick; a *temple* made of precious materials, where God dwells.[25] They are all helpful pictures, but eventually he settled on a metaphor which describes it more dynamically. It is a *body*, of which Christ is the head and we are the members.[26]

A body is healthy when all its parts are healthy and working together for the benefit of the whole. Paul points out how stupid it would be for the eye to say to the hand, or the head to the feet, 'I don't need you'. Each part has a different function, but all the parts serve one another as they work together in the body, under the control of the head. The same applies in the Church. We need each other and Paul stresses that the weaker members are indispensable and, in fact, should be given the 'greater honour'. He tells us that all the parts should have 'equal concern for each other'. For this to happen we clearly must be serving one another. Dietrich Bonhoeffer wrote, 'Every member serves the whole body, either to its health or its destruction.'[27] Serving the Church ('the body' not the structure) is a significant way of serving Christ.

Sometimes a part of the body is suffering or weak. When this happens it is the responsibility of the other members to care for that part until it is restored to health again, just as in the human body. As Paul explained, 'If one part suffers, every part suffers with it; if one part is honoured, every part rejoices with it.'[28] A traditional African proverb puts it, 'The whole body has to bend over to remove a thorn from the foot.' How much do we really care for members of the Church who are suffering in different parts of the world today? Does it move us to action or service in any way?

It is interesting to note that various offices in the Church are designated in terms of servanthood. The word 'minister' (derived from the Latin *minister*) and the term 'deacon' (from the Greek *diakonos*) both mean servant. These offices are concerned with leadership, authority and responsibility, but it is intended that these functions should be expressed in terms of serving others.

This concept applies to all forms of Christian ministry. 'In the New Testament, ministry was a function, not a status. It was a verb, not a noun.'[29]

The word *diakonia,* which means ministry or service, is applied in the Acts of the Apostles to a great range of activities: feeding the hungry (6:1); teaching (6:4); prayer (6:4); giving to needy Christians (11:29); personal service to one Christian by others (19:22); preaching (20:24); evangelism (21:19). Paul used it to describe his whole life of service, when writing of 'the task (*diakonia*) the Lord Jesus has given me' (20:24).

We sometimes think of 'ministry' only in terms of specific Christian service or church related activity. But it includes the whole of who we are and all that we do. Michael Green sums it up: '*Diakonia,* in short, belonged to the whole church and to every member of it. No service was regarded as too menial or exacting if it would commend the Gospel of the grace of God.'[30] No member of the Church is exempt from being a servant. The word *diakonos* is even used to describe our Lord Jesus Christ.[31]

Serving Others

Serving others is a practical expression of our Christian faith, both within and outside the Church. Jesus said that when we serve others in his name, we are serving him, even if it is something as insignificant as giving someone a cup of cold water.[32] In a powerful story that Jesus told of the final judgement when Christ returns, he defines 'the righteous' not in terms of how much faith they had, but by how much their faith had prompted them to respond to the needs of others:

'For I was hungry and you gave me something to eat, I was thirsty and you gave me something to drink, I was a stranger and you invited me in, I needed clothes and you clothed me, I was sick and you looked after me, I was in prison and you came to visit me.'[33]

29

When 'the righteous' were confused as to when they might have seen Jesus in those situations, the Lord explained: 'Whatever you did for one of the least of these brothers of mine, you did for me.'[34]

Theologians have debated since the time of Calvin as to whether the phrase 'these brothers of mine' refers only to poor believers or includes everyone in need. In the context of the parable, it probably does mean primarily the former, but in the light of the whole of Scripture it clearly includes everyone. Jesus told the story of the good Samaritan to make this very point. The command still stands: 'If your enemy is hungry, give him food to eat; if he is thirsty, give him water to drink.'[35]

In 1959 we went to the Sepik Province of Papua New Guinea to set up a hospital and medical programme at Anguganak, a remote jungle area. Our motivation was to serve Christ and make him known to people who had never heard the Good News. 'Serving Christ' turned out to be very different from our expectations. The bulk of the medical work was routine and not very exciting: treating endless cases of malaria, pneumonia, stinking tropical ulcers, scabies, leprosy and tiny babies suffering from extreme malnutrition. Many hours were spent in training medical staff, initially educating people who were barely literate. About a third of our time was spent in caring for the health of missionaries and their families.

A few years later we asked ourselves, is this really what it means to 'serve Christ'? Is this really how we should be serving in this place? There seemed very little 'spiritual fruit' to show for all the effort that we and many other missionaries had poured into the project. There was seldom any expression of gratitude or appreciation from the patients, who had no word for 'thank you' in their language. (Perhaps *yaim* was the closest, meaning 'good'.) But the Lord confirmed to us that this was where he wanted us, and reading Matthew 25 on our knees reinforced it.

In 1999 we returned to Anguganak for the fortieth anniversary celebration of the start of the hospital. To our delight we found a thriving indigenous church, comprised mainly of the next generation. These Christians were not only able to maintain their own spiritual lives and church administration with very little help from missionaries, but were actively reaching out to those in other areas who had never heard the gospel. They thanked us for planting the 'good seed', and assured us that it was bearing fruit . . . '*em i karim planti kaikai nau*'.

DRIVEN OR CALLED?

There is a big difference between serving out of a sense of compulsion and serving out of a sense of call or desire to serve. We all have *internal 'drivers'* that motivate us to do things, often unconsciously, and which can even be behind what appears to be altruistic service. These 'slave-drivers' must be acknowledged and challenged in order for us to be healthy people. In terms of service, they need to be replaced by more appropriate driving forces, such as love for Christ and a servant heart. Here are some common 'drivers' which can be behind our active service:

Guilt

Guilt can be real or false. We may experience *real* guilt, for example, if we promised to do something and have not fulfilled our word. The answer to this, of course, is to admit and confess our failings and then proceed to put them right. However, the feeling of guilt which more often goads us is a *false* guilt, resulting from the expectations or attitudes of others, and the pressure that this places on us. Christian workers may feel guilty because the expectations of others in the church or team do not match up with what they have been called or equipped to do in their service for God. So they may try to meet these unrealistic expectations in order to satisfy others.

Another common situation we have observed in service organisations, whether Christian or secular, is false guilt that members of the team can feel when the leader is an outstanding or competent person. Because he or she is so capable, others feel inadequate by comparison and then guilty because their own work output is much less. So they try to keep up with the leader and often move into burn-out as a result. The leader may never have intended to put this pressure on the team and may be unaware of it, but others have developed a sense of false guilt because while their gifts and abilities are different or not as great, they still try to match the leader's productivity. Service then becomes a duty rather than a pleasure. 'I want to do this' is replaced by 'I have to do it'. The 'May I?' of love becomes the 'Must I?' of duty.[36]

Ambition

Ambition is a strong motivator, but when a selfish ambition to be more successful than others takes over in our service, we move from being a servant of others to serving self. Voluntary service organisations are sometimes plagued by a spirit of competitiveness, pride in personal achievement or jealousy over the success of others. This undermines the value and effectiveness of the service.

Workaholism

A workaholic is someone who has a compulsion to work which causes imbalance in his or her life and often takes precedence over relationships. At times in our lives we may have to work excessively long hours for economic or other unavoidable reasons, but a workaholic chooses to live that way. There are many workaholics in our society, in Christian organisations as well as in business. The root cause of much workaholic behaviour is a lack of self-worth and an attempt to prove one's competence in order to become acceptable and valued by others.

Workaholism has been defined as a special addiction of the religious person, which can become a 'false religion'.[37] Another reason why some people turn to obsessive work is to escape intimacy or conflict in their relationships.[38] When workaholism contaminates service, it erodes the joy that true service brings. On the other hand, Christians may choose to work hard at times out of sheer love and gratitude to the Lord for all he has done for them. This is a valid response, but it is still possible for our 'work for the Lord' to take over our lives in an unbalanced way.

This balance is hard to maintain. We personally find it helpful to step aside periodically and assess our motives for service, spending time in quiet reflection, in order to check whether there are any unhealthy 'drivers' behind what we are doing. Keeping a journal is a helpful tool. Useful questions to ask yourself while writing are: Am I called or driven to do this service? Am I operating out of a sense of guilt and compulsion, or because I love the Lord and those to whom he has called me to be a servant?

We now return to think more about the crisis of service.

CLASH OF VALUES AND WILLS

The value system that Jesus taught is at total variance with the value system of this world. This is certainly true about the issue of greatness. On more than one occasion in Scripture we read that his disciples argued about which of them would be the greatest. After one such argument, Jesus sat down and called them together and said, 'If anyone wants to be first, he must be the very last, and the *servant* of all.' Then he took a little child into his arms and said: 'Whoever welcomes one of these little children in my name welcomes me, and whoever welcomes me does not welcome me but the one who sent me.'[39]

In other words, by welcoming and honouring a child we honour God himself.

In Hebrew thinking in those days, a child was insignificant. For example, a Jewish boy was not a full member of the covenant community until his barmitzvah at twelve. A servant was certainly not more important than the one he served. Yet Jesus identifies these two groups of people as great in God's scale of values.

The disciples clearly had not grasped this truth, because a little while later, two of Jesus's most committed followers came to him and asked for a special favour. They wanted to be identified as chief among his disciples and to have the main places of honour and glory in his coming kingdom. Again Jesus took them all aside and said:

'You know that those who are regarded as rulers of the Gentiles lord it over them, and their high officials exercise authority over them. *Not so with you.* Instead, whoever wants to become great among you must be your *servant*, and whoever wants to be first must be *slave* of all. For even the Son of Man did not come to be served, but to serve, and to give his life as a ransom for many.'[40]

This teaching is just as hard for us to grasp and put into practice today as it was then for the disciples. It goes against the grain and cuts across our human scale of values. Jesus applied this principle not only to us but also to himself, and became the supreme example and model of servanthood. Despite having every right to be served, he came into this world as a servant and was prepared to seal his service with the sacrifice of his life.

On the very last night before going to the cross, either

before or during the last supper, Jesus had to deal with the same issue again. The disciples still had not understood or accepted his teaching and were arguing about who would be the greatest. So Jesus said to them:

'The greatest among you should be like the youngest, and the one who rules like the one who serves. For who is greater, the one who is at the table or the one who serves? Is it not the one who is at the table? But I am among you as one who serves.'[41]

Then he demonstrated this by washing their feet. This menial task was normally expected of a slave or servant. The disciples were not prepared to wash one another's feet, not even the feet of Jesus.[42] They still had not absorbed what Jesus had taught them repeatedly about true greatness.

Have we learned and applied these principles in our lives? This is a question we keep asking ourselves. This teaching of Jesus challenges our personal value system as Christians and is in stark contrast to the way of the world. It just does not make sense to our natural thinking, and so our minds have to be constantly 'renewed'.[43] How much of what we do each day in our 'secular work' or in our 'Christian service' is motivated by self-promotion rather than a true desire to be a servant?

The issue is essentially a matter of our wills. In her classic book, *The Christian's Secret of a Happy Life*, Hannah Smith writes of the struggle of our will against God's. Once this has been settled, 'Obedience is easy and a delight, and service becomes perfect freedom; until the Christian is forced to exclaim, "This happy service! Who could dream the earth had such liberty?"'[44]

SUMMARY

Being a servant is foreign to us and so alien to the values of this world that it takes a lifetime to grasp and apply this principle in our lives. But it is the essence of what it means to follow Jesus. Becoming a servant is how we can best demonstrate true discipleship and God's love to a hurting world.

REFLECTIONS AND EXERCISES

1. GIVING   How much place does giving have in your life? Take some time to reflect in your journal about what you actually give away: of your time, friendship, substance and money. Prayerfully consider whether this is enough, and perhaps ways in which you could increase your giving.
- Record times when giving to others has given you joy and pleasure.
- How easy do you find it to receive the gifts of others?

2. UNCONDITIONAL LOVE   Reflect on how much unconditional love you have received in your life, and how much of it you give to others.
- It could be helpful to study all the references to the word *agapë* in the New Testament (about 120) using a concordance, in order to discover the true meaning and implications of unconditional love.

3. A CALL TO SERVICE   Do you have a sense of call to serve Christ, the church or others? If not, what would help you to obtain this?
- What things in your life might be preventing an awareness of a call to serve?

4. 'DRIVERS'   We all have 'drivers' that make us do certain things and behave in certain ways. Part of maturity is to be able to identify these and deal with them, or at least be aware of them. What 'drivers' are you aware of that may affect your service?
- Re-read the section 'Driven or Called' (p 31) to see if you can identify with any of these 'slave drivers' that might be getting in the way of your service.

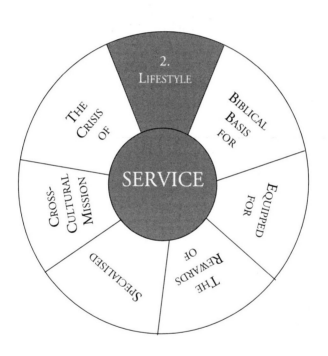

2.
LIFESTYLE

BIBLICAL
BASIS
FOR

THE
CRISIS
OF

EQUIPPED
FOR

SERVICE

CROSS-
CULTURAL
MISSION

THE
REWARDS
OF

SPECIALISED

Two

Lifestyle Service

'Ich dien' – I serve.[1]

Service has been called 'the art of unselfish living', and this affects every aspect of life. Service is often thought of only as a task, but true service flows out of a servant heart and a worldview where life is seen in terms of serving God and others. When this happens, service becomes the natural consequence of living. Subsequent choices will be concerned with deciding which specific service is the right one, rather than a repeated decision to serve. Serving God and others becomes the fulfilment of life rather than an obligation or duty.

FRIENDSHIP

Reaching out and offering friendship to others is a simple yet profound form of service. All human beings need friends in order to develop in a healthy way and find fulfilment and satisfaction in life. Many sociological studies have shown the harmful effects of loneliness and the absence of friends on health and wellbeing.[2] Friendship can be defined as 'a close relationship between two human beings who enjoy each other's company'.[3] There are varying degrees of friendship, from casual acquaintance to close intimacy, but it would be hard to conceive of life without some friendly contact with others. As

39

Aristotle said, 'Without friends no one would choose to live, even if he had all other goods.'[4]

Yet the reality is that many people, especially men, go through life without fulfilling a deep longing for meaningful friendships. Others have a friendship or are in a marriage relationship which falls far below their expectations and desire for closeness. They have an aching void inside which represents their longing to know and be known, to love and be loved. Without others with whom to share their real selves they feel of little value and significance. They may try to fill the void with busyness, material things, an endless round of pleasure-seeking, travel, drugs or perhaps religious activities. But the emptiness remains.

In friendship we can give of ourselves freely to others. C.S. Lewis wrote, 'True friendship is the least jealous of loves.'[5] However, it is not always easy. It involves moving out of my 'world of one' to include someone else, and inevitably invading each other's space in the process. It means taking my attention away from myself and placing it on another; moving from being self-focused to becoming other-focused. This often requires me to give up my felt needs or desires in order to benefit the other person. In the process of adjusting to the lifestyle and values of another I may be hurt. I will certainly be changed. However, friendships also bring with them many rich rewards that make life worth living.

Friendships do not just happen, they require a mutual desire for closeness and a willingness to work at it. Some people do not have the communication skills to build close relationships. Others have tried but have been hurt by broken relationships in the past and so have given up. They consider it safer to hide behind a wall or mask, rather than make themselves vulnerable again. (Principles and skills for building friendships and intimate relationships are outlined in *Created for Intimacy*.[6])

The gift of friendship is one of the greatest acts of service that we can offer and there is no shortage of people needing friends in our world. The paradox is that as we give so we receive; as we offer friendship so we gain a friend. The best way to have a friend is to become a friend and to actively seek to give friendship to someone else. Friendships can be nurtured in many small ways, such as an unexpected phone call; taking time out to have lunch or coffee together; a brief letter or card expressing a caring thought or just a word of encouragement when you meet.

HOSPITALITY

The word 'hospitality' comes from the Latin *hospes*, meaning a host, or a receiver of guests. Becoming a host is usually associated with entertaining people in our homes. This is a simple yet significant way of offering true service to others, especially to those who are in need or unable to entertain us in return.[7] There are numerous stories in the Old and New Testaments which reinforce our obligation to entertain strangers in our home. Jesus said that in caring for and offering hospitality to strangers we are really doing this service for him.[8] 'Don't forget to entertain strangers, for by so doing some people have entertained angels without knowing it.'[9] However, hospitality does not only refer to entertaining others.

The word for enemy in Latin has a similar sound, *hostis*. The art of hospitality is converting *hostis* to *hospes*; turning enemies or strangers into welcome guests. The essence of hospitality is not so much the lavishness of the entertainment as the attitude of the host. True hospitality is given freely as an act of unconditional love, without manipulation or coercion. It is possible to be entertained generously and yet to feel unwelcome, to be fed food but denied fellowship. On the other hand, simple hospitality offered with love and acceptance is a

41

memory which will be treasured by both guest and host. We all have probably experienced this at some time. Solomon said: 'Better a meal of vegetables where there is love than a fattened calf with hatred.'[10] It is recorded that Jesus was invited on more than one occasion to the home of a rich man, out of a hostile rather than hospitable motive.[11] This is in strong contrast to the times he enjoyed the simple hospitality of his friends Lazarus, Martha and Mary.[12]

One Christmas, when we were students in London in our single days, we had nowhere special to go and celebrate the occasion. A couple heard of our dilemma so invited us to share the festivities with them and their two young children. Unfortunately, I (Agnes) was scheduled for duty on Christmas Day, delivering babies in the poorer area of Camden Town.

'Never mind,' they said, 'we'll put off our Christmas dinner until tomorrow so that you can join us.'

When we arrived, we discovered that we were not the only guests. A neighbour who lived on her own and a lonely old man from a rest home nearby had been invited as well. It was one of the happiest Christmas celebrations I can remember. I happened to be looking for new accommodation at the time, and without hesitation they invited me to stay with them as long as I liked. This family opened up not only their home but also their lives to us. They used hospitality as a powerful way of being servants to others.

COMPANIONSHIP

Eating together, hospitality and companionship are closely associated. In fact, the word 'companion' comes from the Latin (*com* = with, *panis* = bread) and we often express friendship by serving food to our guests. This association is particularly important in some cultures, especially in the Middle East, where to invite someone into your home to eat food is not just a casual gesture of friendship, but binds the host to protect his guest while under his roof. Jesus used this significant cultural metaphor to describe his desire to be close to us. He expresses his love and friendship to us in wanting his followers to share regularly in the Communion meal – 'in remembrance of me'.[13] It is significant that each of the Gospel writers emphasises the shock that the disciples expressed when Jesus said that one of them eating the Passover meal with him would also betray him.[14]

In his last message to the seven churches, Jesus applied the metaphor of eating together to describe the relationship he desires with us. He wants to be *our* guest and eat of *our* bread, as well as share his.

> 'Here I am! I stand at the door and knock. If anyone hears my voice and opens the door, I will come in and eat with him, and he will with me.'[15]

Jesus is expressing his longing for true companionship with us. He desires to eat *with us* by sharing the 'bread' of our lives, whatever we want to offer him – our joys, sorrows, struggles, faith, worship – whatever is part of our 'bread'. He also wants us to eat *with him*, to partake of the rich food he has to offer.

In the same way, hospitality is not limited to inviting people into our homes. To be hospitable is to invite people *into our lives*. It is to open ourselves to others. So many people live private lives where there is no room for others, even those they love. This is usually a protection strategy based on fear, because it is risky to invite another to share my inner world. That person will come to know the real me, and this kind of encounter with another might change me, but this is true hospitality. Henri Nouwen described it this way:

Hospitality, therefore, means primarily the creation of free space where the stranger can enter and become a friend instead of an enemy. Hospitality is not to change people, but to offer them space where change can take place. It is not to bring men and women over to our side, but to offer freedom that is not disturbed by dividing lines. It is not to lead our neighbour into a corner where there are no alternatives left, but to open a wide spectrum of options for choice and commitment.[16]

It is not possible to offer this quality of hospitality to everyone in our lives. Some people do not want it, even in their close relationships. Real intimacy is too threatening for them. In the early years of our marriage, we were unable to share fully at this level. We have discovered since that a rich relationship can only develop when two people take the risk of 'eating one another's bread'. It is also fulfilling to have this kind of relationship with a number of people, perhaps at different levels. True hospitality is a mutually rewarding experience of service.

MARRIAGE

There is no better situation in which to learn how to serve than in a marriage relationship, as we have discovered over the past forty-six years. Christian marriage calls for mutual servanthood, not just occasionally when the mood takes us, but twenty-four hours a day. The New Testament definition of marriage is found in Ephesians 5:21, where Paul instructs couples to '*Submit to one another* out of reverence for Christ' (emphasis ours). Submitting to another is the essence of service. Paul clearly gives the command to *both* the husband and the wife to submit to each other, because Christ is the head of a Christian home. Mutual submission is not a problem when we give Christ his rightful place as Lord of our relationship.

44

In our English translations, the word 'submit' also occurs in verse 22: 'Wives, submit to your husbands as to the Lord', but it is *not there* in the Greek text (though it is implied). Paul did not need to tell wives to submit in that culture, because both Hebrew and Greek wives were virtual slaves of their husbands. A wife was her husband's property. If she displeased him in some way he could divorce her, but she could not divorce him. So he is not telling wives to submit to their husbands so much as telling them *how* to do it – not out of bitterness or resentment, but 'as to the Lord'.

In the same way he instructs husbands: 'Love your wives, just as Christ loved the church and gave himself up for her' (v 25). He does not remind wives to love their husbands, because by definition Christians are those who love one another.[17] In fact, he is not telling husbands to love their wives so much as describing the *quality* of the love required – even to death, as modelled by Jesus.

Mutual submission is worked out in practice through mutual servanthood, based on mutual love. When Jesus said, 'Love your neighbour as you love yourself', this must apply in the first instance in marriage, where husbands and wives are each other's nearest neighbour. Paul makes this point again in verses 28 and 33. Being a servant to one another is a reflection of the quality of our love, and keeps a marriage relationship in proper balance. Many years ago, we came across a statement which we have built into our relationship and which helps us keep this principle of mutual submission in perspective: 'I will always be your servant, but you will never be my master.' The mutuality of serving one another in marriage doubles the joy of sharing life together.

PARENTING

Loving parents become servants to their children. This is the nature of parenting. It certainly is for the first two decades or so of their young lives. Tiny babies have everything done for them – they are held, fed, bathed, entertained. Parents not only wash their children's feet, but also their bottoms! Observant mothers learn to interpret their infant's 'language', and will respond in different ways to the various types of cry their child makes.

As children grow, they begin to develop independence, but still take up enormous amounts of their care-giver's time, especially in their early years. In our modern lifestyle, many parents spend countless hours as 'taxi drivers' for their children, taking them to various cultural, social and sporting activities. Above all, children need quality time spent with them by both parents. This is how they know they are loved. As it has been said, children spell love T-I-M-E. Many parents are willing to give their children 'things' but not time.

Another reason why parents need to spend a lot of time with their children is to understand them in order to be able to train them adequately. Each child is different, and it takes time to discover who each one is in his or her uniqueness.

Solomon made a very profound statement in this regard: 'Train a child in the way he should go, and when he is old he will not turn from it.'[18] Proverbs are not promises but probabilities. This statement does not guarantee that children will follow the right way if we have trained them the best way we know how. Children will eventually choose their own way, and many influences affect this choice. However, it is saying that time spent in proper training is likely to pay off in the long run. The important inference of this proverb (which is often missed) is the point that each child is different and so must be trained 'in the way *he/she should go*'.

In other words, the training must be tailored in a way that is right for that particular child, not necessarily in the way the parents may have assumed the child should go. To discover the child's own uniqueness takes time, and also requires humility and much wisdom from God. The reverse style of making all of life's decisions for a child rather than with him or her is counter-productive

Good parenting involves being servants to our children. Parents model the message of servanthood to their children, so that they in turn will be servants to their children. However, this message must be 'taught' as well as 'caught'. The principles of mutual submission and mutual servanthood apply to the family as well as to the marriage. There must be a balance in this. Some children have learned to treat their parents as slaves. Other children grow up in families where they are used by their parents as virtual slaves. In functional families, the children take increasing responsibility for being servants by caring for their parents as they grow older. If mutual servanthood has been modelled and taught when the family is young, this reversal of roles becomes a natural sequence. Kahlil Gibran has expressed some of these thoughts about children in a beautiful poem:

> And a woman who held a babe against her bosom said,
> Speak to us of Children. And he said:
> Your children are not your children.
> They are the sons and daughters of Life's longing for itself.
> They come through you but not from you,
> And though they are with you yet they belong not to you.
>
> You may give them your love but not your thoughts
> For they have their own thoughts.
> You may house their bodies but not their souls,
> For their souls dwell in the house of tomorrow, which
>   you cannot visit, not even in your dreams.

You may strive to be like them, but seek not to make
   them like you.
For life goes forward not backward nor tarries with
   yesterday.

You are the bows from which your children as living
   arrows are sent forth.
The Archer sees the mark upon the path of the infinite,
   and He bends you with His might so that His
   arrows go swift and far.
Let your bending in the Archer's hand be for gladness;
For even as He loves the arrow that flies,
   so He loves the bow that is stable.[19]

The metaphor of children being like arrows, parents the bow and God the Archer, is from an ancient song attributed to Solomon:

Sons (and daughters) are a heritage from the LORD,
   children a reward from him.
Like arrows in the hands of a warrior
   are sons born in one's youth.
Blessed is the man whose quiver is full of them.[20]

I (John) have a fascination for arrows. I've spent many hours sitting around smoky village fires in Papua New Guinea, watching men skilfully prepare their arrows from straight pieces of bamboo. The tips are carved out of hard wood or bone and carefully fitted to the end of the shaft and bound on with strips of vine. Arrow heads are designed in many ways, depending whether the intended target is a bird, a fish, a pig or perhaps a human being. I've also spent many hours removing arrowheads from bodies, some of which had been there for a long time. So

I was curious to understand why children are described as arrows.

The message became clear: although we may have a number of 'arrows' in our 'quiver', they are not meant to stay there. Children are precious gifts, but they are not our possession. They are on loan, for us to love and train and prepare to be shot forth into the world like an arrow. The responsibility of the 'bow' is to point them at the right target. This is not easy, and that is why we need the help of the Archer to hold the bow steady and stable. The main task of parenting is to prepare our children for the time when we let them go. We only have one shot. There are no re-runs.

When it comes to family life, a focus on service must be kept in balance. On the one hand, there is a danger that family demands will take over, leaving parents little time to reach out to others in love and care. Then there is also the reverse danger of the family being neglected in the interests of others. Many missionary couples have agonised over this, trying to find the right balance between the needs of their children and the demands of their calling. This is one of the biggest problems in overseas missionary service. We have met numerous 'Mish Kids' (Third Culture people) who felt deprived of their parents' time and attention by the demands of the missionary task. Some became so bitter about it that they turned away from their faith in later life.

This is not just a problem of overseas service, but also in the homeland. One woman told us she remembers as a child sitting in the car for hours on the way home from school, while her mother did her 'servant thing' for friends and neighbours. Other children have grown up resentful of their minister father, or doctor parent, who always appeared to have more time for parishioners or patients than for them. There is no quick answer to this problem, and each family must face the issue together and find their own solutions. However, there are some principles which we found helpful in making decisions:

- Have a clear order of priorities for your goals in life. For us, we learned to put family before our work, whatever that work may be. There will be times when this rule has to be broken, but we regard this priority as the 'norm'. Paul's instruction to Timothy in this regard is challenging: 'If anyone does not *provide* for his family, and especially for his immediate family, he has denied the faith and is worse than an unbeliever.'[21] The Greek word translated 'provide' means 'to take thought for' or 'have regard for'. This means much more than being a good provider for the family's physical needs. It includes giving time and thought to our children's emotional, social and spiritual needs and development as well. This is harder to do and is more time consuming.
- Include the children as far as possible in any decision-making when it involves the family. This makes the hard decisions affecting them more bearable, and they appreciate being included in what mum and dad are doing for the Lord.
- Remember that Jesus promised great rewards to family members, both parents and children, who have had to make sacrifices for his sake.[22]

GRANDPARENTING

The problem with being a parent is that you don't know much about it until the job is over. Being a grandparent can provide a second chance to make up for some of our mistakes in parenting. We are grateful for fifteen such opportunities. The grandparent–grandchild relationship is something special. For one thing, you are likely to have more time to give than parents, who are often busy building a career. Because of the pressures of life, parents are sometimes operating in 'survival mode'. This makes giving adequate time to their children difficult.

By the time you are a grandparent, you have hopefully gained a lot more wisdom than you had thirty or so years earlier. Caring for grandchildren takes time and energy, but at the end of the day or weekend you know you can hand them back! Relating to grandchildren helps to keep you young in heart and mind. You will be constantly amazed by the wonder and wisdom of a little child. The generation gap is wider than with your children, so this calls for tolerance and a willingness to learn from them as well as teach. This relationship requires time and patience, but is incredibly rewarding and provides another opportunity to experience again the joy of service. A grandparent with a grandchild on their knee can't help reflecting on the truth Jesus taught:

'Anyone who takes care of a little child like this is caring for me! And whoever cares for me is caring for God who sent me. Your care for others is the measure of your greatness.'[23]

HEALING

We live in a broken world, surrounded by pain and sickness of mind and body. We can respond to suffering or choose to do nothing about it, but it is not possible to ignore it. Suffering and sickness are part of being human, and will affect all of us at some time or another; how we respond to it, both in our own experience and in the lives of others, says a lot about who we are as people. Responding lovingly and creatively to the suffering that people around us experience is a servant attitude. There is and always will be a great need for the service of healing in our churches and communities. We can all bring healing to others.

Reaching out with compassion and comfort is the Christian response to suffering. As we pointed out in the last chapter with regard to giving, comfort is also a two-way process. When we have been comforted we are able to comfort others, and as we comfort others so we will be comforted. Paul expressed it this way: '[God] comforts us in all our troubles, so that we can comfort those in any trouble with the comfort we ourselves have received from God.'[24]

Avenues of Healing

There are many ways in which we can become servant-healers and offer comfort to others. Perhaps the most obvious is through one of the many branches of the medical or nursing professions. Jesus modelled the service of healing throughout his ministry and instructed his followers to do the same.[25] The book of Acts describes how the apostles took this command seriously, and the Church has led the way in providing hospitals and healing down through the centuries. This form of service still attracts a high proportion of Christians into its ranks as an avenue through which to serve Christ and express compassion and love. Of course, countless men and women who have no Christian commitment also serve their fellow human beings in the healing professions.

Mental and emotional healing is just as important as physical healing, and much more attention was paid to these aspects in the second half of the twentieth century. There is a greater understanding of mental illness and a more humane, balanced approach to the treatment and management of people with psychiatric disorders. However, mental illness is still feared, and is less 'acceptable' in many societies than physical illness.

Emotional disorders also have received more attention over

the past forty years or so, with an increasing acceptance and use of counselling in the community. Skilled professional counselling has a lot to offer people who suffer from depression, anxiety, emotional disorders, trauma experienced in childhood or in later life, and relationship problems. In our counselling work, we have moved away from a focus on 'problem counselling' to '*growth counselling*'. By this we mean helping people know themselves better and develop maturity and life skills, which will empower them to deal with their own problems. The aim is to provide 'tools' rather than solutions.

There are many other forms of people-care which can be included under the service of healing, such as: social work, care of the aged, looking after people who are physically or intellectually impaired, helping refugees. Some of these services may not seem so attractive or dramatic as being able to provide medical or emotional healing, but they are just as vital to the welfare of society. Addressing the many social problems in the community, especially in big cities; working to provide better housing; improving the food supply for the two thirds of the world's population who go to bed hungry each night, are all ways of bringing healing to suffering humanity. Some of the healing professions are discussed in Chapter Six.

Dangers of Being a Healer

It is a healthy exercise to periodically examine our motives, even for something as noble as healing or relieving suffering. It is possible to become a healer of other's hurts in order to feel needed and fulfilled ourselves. One day our motives will be revealed. 'He will bring to light what is hidden in darkness and will expose the motives of men's hearts. At that time each will receive his praise from God.'[26]

For people who have a burden to relieve suffering and be involved in a healing ministry, there is always the danger of becoming 'rescuers'. To do things for people can sometimes be disempowering. It is far better to work *with* them in achieving their goal. To do things for people which they could or should do for themselves builds dependence. True love does not smother, limit or control another person. Rather, it encourages independence and responsibility. Paul made some perceptive comments about this:

> Carry each other's burdens, and in this way you will fulfil the law of Christ. If anyone thinks he is something when he is nothing, he deceives himself. Each one should test his own actions. Then he can take pride in himself without comparing himself to somebody else, for each one should carry his own load.[27]

The 'law of Christ' refers to Jesus' command to love one another.[28] This is the motivation of our service. The word 'carry' is better translated 'share'.[29] None of us is called upon to be the world's burden-bearer; only Christ is. The word translated 'burden' here is the Greek word *baros*, which means a heavy load, such as a slave or burden-bearer was expected to carry. When people are under a heavy load, we are called upon to share it with them, not to take it from them.

At the end of this passage, Paul states that we all have our own 'load' to carry. This is a different word, *phortion*, which means your pack. Each soldier in an army has his own seventy-pound pack to carry, but is sometimes called upon to share another's burden. So too with carers and healers. We are called upon to share another's heavy burden but not to take it from him or her and add it to our own load. We all have our own packs to carry.

An understanding of this has been vital to us in our counselling practice. There were times when we were tempted to carry burdens that were brought to us. For example, when working with a couple struggling in their marriage relationship, we found ourselves assuming the responsibility of bringing their marriage together. We even felt guilty if it didn't work out. We had to learn that their relationship was entirely *their* responsibility. Our task was to provide the best counselling help we could. However much we wanted to see their marriage come together again, we could not do the work for them. We are responsible *to* our clients but are not responsible *for* them.

If we had continued taking on other people's burdens, instead of helping them to carry them, we would have moved into 'burnout'. We have worked with a number of counsellors, 'healers' and Christian workers who have burned out for this very reason. This is one of the main factors accounting for the condition now defined as 'compassion fatigue'.[30]

The Wounded Healer

We have all been hurt by life's experiences and each of us has a *wounded* part. To be wounded within is an inevitable part of life. We all have within us our '*healing*' or 'shalom' as well. This is that part of us which longs for health and wholeness in ourselves and others. However, my woundedness will only respond to my own inner healer in conjunction with God's healing power. Your healer cannot heal my wound, nor can mine restore yours.

How then can we become agents of healing for one another? David Augsburger explains this well in his book, *Pastoral Counselling Across Cultures*[31] and Figure 2:1 sets out the process in a visual form. This model is helpful in understanding the healing process, particularly for counselling, but it applies to all forms of healing.

Healers operate best out of their woundedness and vulnerability. In their desire to help others, healers sometimes deny or try to hide their own wounds. If we do this, we will be less effective as healers and may come across as being unreal or phoney. This does not mean that we should display our wounds in an exhibitionist way. We may not even refer to them, but we operate more effectively if we are in touch with them. Henri Nouwen writes in *The Wounded Healer*, 'Making one's own wounds a source of healing does not call for a sharing of superficial personal pains but for a constant willingness to see one's own pain and suffering as arising from the depth of the human condition.'[32]

• If 'healer' and 'sufferer' meet *wound to wound* (Figure 2:1 B) this results in a release of sympathy from the healer. This is not a bad thing in itself, but an overly sympathetic response will reduce our effectiveness as healers. We may be swamped by our own pain, and will probably increase the pain of the other. Of course, 'No one can help anyone without becoming involved, without entering with his whole person into the painful situation, without taking the risk of becoming hurt, wounded or even destroyed in the process.'[33] The healer must feel sympathy and compassion for the sufferer, but this must be tempered by a degree of objectivity. This is particularly so in the decisions that need to be made in medical practice. For example, if doctors or nurses are overwhelmed by the tragedy or pain of the sufferer, they will be less able to offer effective help.

• If they connect 'healing' to 'wound' (Figure 2:1 C) this may seem ideal, but it is also fraught with problems. It lays the healer open to the dangers outlined in the last section. The healer may become a 'rescuer' and the sufferer a dependent victim. This disempowers the sufferer, and will block his or her inner healing process. Dependency and paternalism are real dangers that healers must be aware of and seek to avoid. True

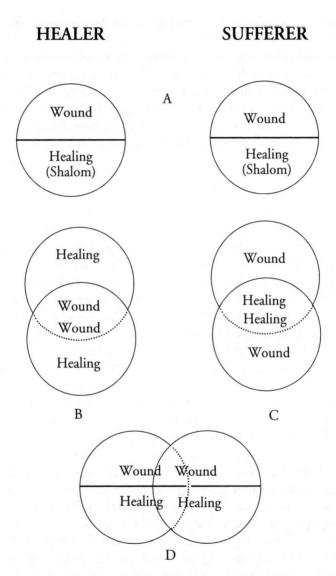

Fig. 2:1. Interactions of Healer and Sufferer[34]

healing empowers others and does not leave them feeling dependent on the healer.

The best healing involves doing things *with* people rather than for them. When Jesus healed, he placed great emphasis on the sufferer's faith. In fact, on three occasions he said: '*Your faith has made you whole.*'[35] Healing in these instances was a co-operative process. In the same way, healers should come alongside and help people resolve their problems, rather than try to solve the problems for them.

• The ideal connection is when healer and sufferer meet *wound to wound and healer to healer* (Figure 2:1 D). This is based on empathy more than sympathy. The healer will not now contaminate the sufferer's wound by his own pain, but will draw out the healing forces within the other. 'When meeting healing to healing (as well as wound to wound) the illusion that wholeness can be given by one person to another is dispelled. Healing is not a gift to be given, it is a life awakened, strengthened, nourished.'[36]

This model of healing is what the Lord himself, the Wounded Healer showed us: 'He was pierced for our transgressions, he was crushed for our iniquities; the punishment that brought us peace was upon him, and *by his wounds we are healed.*'[37] Let us learn from our Master how we too can become wounded healers, and be his agents in a hurting world. Ask the Lord to show you today how to share the healing you have received with someone who is lonely, discouraged, afraid, sick or in prison. Opportunities are there all around us.

PRAYER

Service and prayer go together, like the rhythm of walking: first one foot then the other – the left foot is prayer, the right foot is service. We can't walk without using both feet, and one of them is not more important than the other. Jesus modelled this in his life. He covered every day and every situation with prayer, and no action was performed without intimate contact with his Father. In an active life of service, sometimes we give prayer a secondary place. John Wesley wrote in his journal, 'I have so much to do today I need to spend an extra hour in prayer.' This is not easy to put into practice, but is the source of effective service

'The primary purpose of prayer is not for our own needs to be met, nor for our own desires to be satisfied, but to glorify God in the way we pray and live.'[38]

In asking for prayer for himself, Paul doesn't request what we might expect, that he would be released from prison, but that he would fearlessly proclaim the gospel.[39] Paul cared more about his service for God and the work of the kingdom than his own life.

The Mystery of Prayer

How to pray effectively is our dilemma until we learn to pray as Jesus prayed. The Holy Spirit helps us in our prayers because we don't know how we should pray.[40] We can't understand how our prayers can be effective, but God has called us to share in this mystery of prayer and intercession for others. Often in our prayers we are guilty of telling God what *we* want him to do for others. We don't know the whole story and the wider picture of people's lives and circumstances. It can sometimes be more worthwhile just to reflectively lift up the name of the individual before God for his blessing

Sometimes our prayers become like a 'shopping list', ticking off the items as we locate them on the shelves of the supermarket of needs. True prayer is deeper than that. It means empathising with those we pray for, entering into their struggles, and holding them up to God to do what *he* wants.

His plans for them are immeasurably more than we in our limited way can ask or imagine.[41]

Prayer as Service

We not only pray for ourselves and our service for God, but for other people. Paul reminds us to 'never stop praying, especially for others'.[42] In the body of Christ, we are called to serve one another not only in action but also through prayer. Prayer is a powerful form of service. In intercessory prayer we need to take time to 'see' the one we are praying for, to 'hear' their pain and need, and translate that into seeking God's will for them. 'Compassion lies at the heart of intercession.'[43] So prayer as service is being in the spirit of prayer, dependent on God as we bring people and their needs to him in faith. In this way our service can glorify God and enrich the world in which we live.

SUMMARY

The concept of service includes all of our life and relationships. It is not only an action but an attitude; it is a way of life as well as an activity. Service starts at home in the way we treat our partners, children and grandchildren. It determines the quality of friendships we have, the effectiveness of our healing ministry in the lives of others and it can be powerfully expressed in our prayer life. When service becomes a way of life we receive far more than we give.

REFLECTIONS AND EXERCISES

1. FRIENDSHIP   Write down a list of your friends. Does it include people you have deliberately tried to reach out to because you've been aware of their need of friendship? How have they responded?
- Are there other people you know who would welcome your friendship?

2. HOSPITALITY   How important is it for you to entertain others in your home? How often have you offered hospitality in the past six months? Would you like to increase this?
- Remember that true hospitality means inviting people into your life. How open are you to sharing deeply with others? Would you like to develop this skill?
- It could be useful to write in your journal about this.

3. MARRIAGE   To what degree are 'mutual submission' and 'mutual servanthood' operating in your relationship? How has this affected the amount of intimacy that you experience?
- Discuss this together with your spouse, in the light of Ephesians 5:21–33.
- What changes would you both like to make?
- How has the model of servanthood that you have shown affected the lives of your children and/or grandchildren?
- The concept and outworking of mutual submission could make a valuable discussion topic for a family and an opportunity to develop greater closeness.

4. HEALING   What avenues of healing are you already involved in? In what other ways could you reach out as a 'healing servant' to others?

- Discuss with a friend or in a small group the concept of 'the wounded healer' and how this applies in your lives?

5. PRAYER Is prayer a vital part of your life as you seek to serve God? In what ways could you plan to develop your prayer life?
- To what degree are you seeking to serve others through prayer? How could you increase this ministry of intercession, either on your own or in partnership with another?

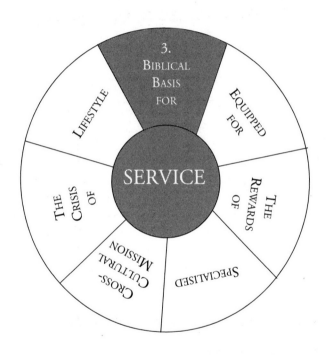

3.
BIBLICAL
BASIS
FOR

EQUIPPED
FOR

LIFESTYLE

SERVICE

THE
REWARDS
OF

THE
CRISIS
OF

CROSS-
CULTURAL
MISSION

SPECIALISED

Three

Biblical Basis for Service

'Serve one another in love'
Paul[1]

Service and work are creation values, and were part of God's plan for humankind from the dawn of time. God is constantly at work in the world. We read that after completing his creation, 'God had finished the work he had been doing; so on the seventh day he rested from all his work'.[2] This was not because he was tired but that he might enjoy his creation. As human beings are created in the image of God, we too have been designed to enjoy working creatively. In fact, we are told that 'The LORD God took the man and put him in the Garden of Eden *to work* it and take care of it'; meaning 'to *serve* and preserve it'.[3]

A BIBLICAL PERSPECTIVE ON WORK

The Dignity of Work

The Greek philosophers taught that manual work had low status and was fit only for slaves, that it was beneath the dignity of free persons. To Aristotle, leisure was the goal of life, and Socrates taught that working in the trades discouraged friendship and citizenship. This is at odds with the Judaeo–Christian ethic which dignifies manual labour as a gift from God and good for our well-being. Adam was a gardener and his two sons specialised in animal husbandry and agriculture. All kinds of craftsmanship were developed early on in the history of human achievements,[4] and we read that Bezalel was 'filled with the Spirit of God, with skill, ability and knowledge in all kinds of crafts' as a jeweller.[5] The Bible is full of images of God at work; for example, he is described as: Creator, Shepherd, Architect and Builder, Potter, Tailor, Gardener and Orchardist.[6]

God is portrayed as a builder who wants to work *together with us* to build our lives and homes: 'Unless the LORD builds the house, its builders labour in vain.'[7] The Hebrew word used here for house is *bayith*, meaning a building but also a home or household. From the context of this psalm, 'house' clearly refers to family relationships. Even though God is described as building the house or home, it is 'the builders' (the parents) who do the work of creating and developing a family. God is the Architect and Master Builder who guides and inspires all our building work. The clear implication of this statement is that God wants to be involved in whatever we are building. Paul defined Christians as 'God's fellow-workers'.[8] God is constantly at work in his world and he invites us to join him and work together with him.

Jesus himself spent more of his life in manual work as a carpenter than he did as a teacher. He regarded the work God had given him to do as very important: 'My food is to do the will of him who sent me and to finish his work.' and 'My Father is always at his work to this very day, and I, too, am working.'[9]

Paul modelled the importance of manual labour by earning his living through tent-making at the same time as he was working as a missionary.[10] This followed the normal Jewish practice of the time when it was expected that rabbis, or teachers, also had a trade. Paul taught that all Christians should be known as people who worked with their own hands.[11] He instructed Titus to encourage others to 'Be ready for any honest work'.[12]

A Christian Work Ethic

There is a need today to think through a truly Christian perspective on work. A common attitude in our society is that work is merely an unfortunate necessity and its only purpose is to make money. There has been a growing demand throughout the last century for increased leisure time. Some people use this extra time as an opportunity to work for more money. Others fill their leisure hours with recreation, or playing with their expensive 'toys' that often require a lot of work to maintain! For many, work has become a religion or idol leading to workaholism. Work controls their lives, not for its own value but for the financial gain, or sense of power or prestige that follows. (See comments in Chapter One on workaholism.)

The Renaissance writers asserted the dignity of physical labour and especially valued the work of one's hands. The Reformation leaders rejected the artificial division between sacred and secular work that had grown up over the centuries. They taught that all work was of equal, intrinsic value and affirmed the biblical principle that it was to be done 'to the glory of God'.[13] They believed that work was a means of serving God and society, and taught that we should see our work or profession as a calling. Some Christians would debate this last point and prefer to see their calling, or vocation, as serving God. (Vocation comes from the Latin *vocare*, meaning 'to call'.) They regard their profession as the means by which they express their primary calling. For example, we see ourselves not as a doctor and nurse who are Christians, but Christians who happen to be a doctor and a nurse. Our vocation is to serve Christ within the medical profession.

Stewardship

Another important Christian perspective is to see work in terms of stewardship. Jesus explores this concept in the parable of the talents.[14] The master went away and entrusted his property and money to his servants to manage. We too have been entrusted with personal and material 'talents' and resources, along with life and strength with which to use them. 'Applied to work, it means that the work we perform in the world is given to us by God. To accomplish our work is to serve God.'[15] God looks for faithful service, though he gives us the freedom to choose to serve him or not. The servants in the parable were judged on the basis of the *faithfulness* of their service. Their rewards were their master's praise for faithful service, being able to share his happiness and an opportunity for greater service.

How does our work relate to our faith? Work and worship have often been regarded by Christians as two separate functions, or different aspects of serving God. Is this consistent with biblical perspectives?

SERVICE AND WORSHIP

The concepts of service and worship are interrelated and almost interchangeable in Scripture. The Hebrew word *abad,* meaning to serve, is related to the idea of working but also has the meaning of worship. For example, God called Moses to bring the Israelites to 'serve God upon this mountain' (AV),[16] which is also translated 'worship God on this mountain' (NIV). They were not required to perform any service or work there, only to worship God. However, it is understandable that Pharaoh felt threatened when Moses told him that God demanded that he should 'let my people go, that they may serve me'.[17] After all, Pharaoh regarded them as his servants and he wasn't about to let them go to serve someone else.

The same link between service and worship is found in the New Testament. The Greek word *latreuö*, which is used primarily of hired service, is also used to describe spiritual service or worship in connection with the priests serving in the temple.[18] As Christians, our bodies are the temple of the Holy Spirit, and so Paul tells us to offer our 'bodies as living sacrifices, holy and pleasing to God which is your spiritual worship' (*latreia*) or 'reasonable service' (AV).[19] The same applies to the word *leitourgeö* which is used interchangeably for service and worship.[20] Someone has coined the word 'workship' to convey the meaning!

Service and worship are not to be separated. Work is sometimes regarded as a purely secular activity and worship an unrelated spiritual function. This is not healthy nor is it a helpful division of our lives. Our service for God in the world should arise from and be concurrent with our worship of God. Thomas Kelly wrote that we need 'ways of conducting our inward life so that we are perpetually bowed in worship while we are also very busy in the world of daily affairs'.[21]

This is not easy, especially for those of us who have been brought up with a western, work-driven ethos, but it is integral to being a servant of the Lord. It requires a change in attitude and perspective on life. Brother Lawrence described this in his little book, *The Practice of the Presence of God*. He worshipped God while he cleaned pots and pans in the kitchen as much as during set times for prayer and devotions. 'The time of business does not with me differ from the time of prayer.' In his daily work he enjoyed 'an habitual, silent and secret conversation of the soul with God'.[22] This is summed up in the words of Horatius Bonar's lovely hymn: 'Fill Thou my life, O Lord my God, in every part with praise'. The hymn concludes:

So shall no part of day or night
From sacredness be free
But all my life in every step
Be fellowship with Thee.[23]

Within the body of Christ there are different functions; some people are gifted as leaders and some are followers. Some are called to be pastors and shepherds of the flock and others are the ones who are led, but the same principles of service apply to us all as we work together for the kingdom of God.

SERVICE AND LEADERSHIP

One of the greatest needs in the Church today is for effective spiritual leaders. Jesus was in the business of training leaders when he chose the twelve apostles. In Matthew 23 we have his clear teaching about the kind of leaders he was looking for. Most commentators believe this section was addressed primarily to his disciples rather than to the crowd.

The chapter opens with Jesus denouncing the false leadership shown by the teachers of the law and Pharisees of his day. They loved to be greeted in the market places as 'Rabbi' or 'Teacher' and always chose the important seats in the synagogue or at feasts. They demanded total obedience from their followers, but Jesus said that 'they do not practise what they preach' (v 3). In this chapter are the harshest words of Jesus ever recorded, uttered against false leaders who placed heavy burdens on the backs of their followers.

The issue at stake was not whether or not they were leaders, but that their attitudes were wrong. They insisted on being called 'Rabbi', 'Father', 'Master' and 'Teacher'. In verses 8–11 Jesus said that they should not seek such titles, 'for you have only one Master and you are all brothers. Do not call anyone on earth "father", for you have one Father and he is in heaven.'

It is clear from the context that Jesus is not prohibiting the use of titles per se, but pointing out that there is no place in leadership for arrogance, pride and the abuse of power. Every leader is identified by some title, but this is to indicate function and not superior status. The leaders in the early church were identified as 'apostles', 'elders' and 'deacons'.

In this context Jesus made the point: 'The greatest among you will be your servant. For whoever exalts himself will be humbled, and whoever humbles himself will be exalted' (vv 11,12). True spiritual leadership is *servant-leadership*. Authority given to spiritual leaders is always under God. Servant leaders do not focus on their own needs but on those of others. His or her desire is to uphold and encourage the followers. This contrasted starkly with the practice of the day, where disciples of the Pharisees never walked beside their teacher as this would indicate equality.

Jesus reversed this attitude by what he taught, but he also modelled his teaching by his life. We turn now to look in more detail at the example he set.

JESUS, THE SERVANT KING

'If there is one word to sum up the ministry of Jesus, it is *service*.'[24] The disciples of Jesus found this hard to understand. They were expecting a conquering Messiah who would dispose of their Roman masters and restore the fortunes of Israel.[25] Their picture did not include service, suffering and death. On one occasion James and John asked if they could be given positions of honour and sit on each side of Christ in his glory. When the other ten disciples heard about it they were indignant. So Jesus called them together and explained what it was like in his kingdom.

'[The] rulers of the Gentiles lord it over them, and their

high officials exercise authority over them. *Not so with you.* Instead, whoever wants to become great among you must be your servant, and whoever wants to be first must be slave of all. For *even the Son of Man did not come to be served, but to serve,* and to give his life a ransom for many.'[26]

As we saw in Chapter One, Jesus turned their value system, and ours, upside down in terms of understanding power and authority.

The Perfect Servant

Jesus applied the principle of being a servant not only to his disciples but also to himself. Matthew identifies Jesus as God's chosen servant, who 700 years earlier Isaiah had prophesied would come:

Here is my servant whom I have chosen, the one I love, in whom I delight; I will put my Spirit on him, and he will proclaim justice to the nations. He will not quarrel or cry out; no-one will hear his voice in the streets. A bruised reed he will not break, and a smouldering wick he will not snuff out, till he leads justice to victory.[27]

Paul describes this incredible step that Jesus took in mind-boggling and powerful words that were probably used as a credal statement or hymn by the early Christians:

Your attitude should be the same as that of Christ Jesus: Who, being in very nature God, did not consider equality with God something to be grasped, but made himself nothing, taking the very nature of a servant, being made in human likeness. And being found in appearance as a

man, he humbled himself and became obedient to death
– even death on a cross![28]

The Greek word translated 'servant' here is *doulos,* meaning
a slave. A slave is someone whose whole life is totally in the
possession of another, including his will. Jesus said, 'I have
come down from heaven not to do my will but to do the will
of him who sent me.'[29] Our Lord is not asking us his servants
to do anything that he himself has not done already. Humility
and obedience are the hallmarks of true servants.

The Gospel records give eloquent testimony to the fact that
Jesus lived his life as a servant. He reached out to the sick, the
weak and marginalised in society. We read that he was often
moved with compassion towards individuals and the crowds.[30]
The Greek word used for the compassion of Jesus means to be
moved to action from one's inner bowels, or heart, not just out
of a sense of pity or duty. Jesus gave himself unstintingly to his
disciples, to the demanding crowds and especially to those in
need. Even in his intense suffering on the cross, Jesus was still
concerned for the needs of his mother, the people of Jerusalem
and the thieves who were dying with him, rather than his own
pain.[31]

The Suffering Servant

Jesus also fulfilled the prophecies of Isaiah given some seven
hundred years earlier about the Servant-Messiah who would
have to suffer:

> *My servant* will act wisely; he will be raised and lifted up
> and highly exalted . . . his appearance was so disfigured
> beyond that of any man and his form marred beyond
> human likeness . . . a man of sorrows, and familiar with
> suffering . . . Surely he took up our infirmities and carried

our sorrows . . . After the suffering of his soul, he will see the light of life and be satisfied; by his knowledge *my righteous servant* will justify many, and will bear their iniquities.[32]

Jesus was aware that his chosen destiny was to come to earth as a man; to serve and suffer in order to fulfil the Father's will.

The Servant-Teacher

Jesus modelled servanthood for the three years he was with his disciples, but they were slow to get the message. It seems that they frequently argued, even at the last supper, about which of them should be the greatest.[33] This was the final evening Jesus would be with them before he died. He had so much to share with them but he had to begin all over again to teach them about being servants. So he wrapped a towel around his waist, poured water into a basin and began to wash his disciples' dusty feet, drying them with the towel.[34]

To see their Master take on the role of a junior slave and wash their feet must have silenced all conversation, as Jesus washed twelve pairs of dusty feet, including those of Judas, who was about to betray him. The task would have taken him at least half an hour. True to form, Peter broke the silence in protest as he found the thought of Jesus washing his feet so humbling and revolutionary. But he certainly learned the lesson that day, and many years later he wrote: '[Be] eager to serve . . . clothe yourselves with humility . . . Humble yourselves, therefore, under God's mighty hand.'[35]

Finally, Jesus resumed his seat again and said: 'Do you understand what I have done for you? . . . You call me "Teacher" and "Lord", and rightly so, for that is what I am. Now that I, your Lord and Teacher, have washed your feet, you also should wash one another's feet. I have set you an example that you should do as I have done for you.'[36] That message is just as real for us today, and just as hard for us to put into practice. We are called to serve one another.

Maybe the disciples remembered the parable Jesus had taught earlier, parts of which he now acted out in the upper room: 'Be dressed and ready for service and keep your lamps burning.' He goes on to say that when the master returns 'he will dress himself to serve, will have them recline at the table and will come and wait on them'.[37] Again, Jesus was not asking them, or us, to do what he had not demonstrated himself. The message is clear, those who want to follow Jesus prove it by servanthood.

Serving out of Fullness not Emptiness

There is a significant statement at the start of the account of Jesus washing his disciples' feet. In verse 3 of John 13 we read, 'Jesus knew that the Father had put all things under his power, and that he had come from God and was returning to God.' He knew exactly who he was, where he had come from and where he was going. Jesus was totally confident of his identity and destiny, and so he served his disciples as a slave out of a place of strength, not weakness. He served out of fullness, not emptiness.

This has important applications for us. If we lack clear identity and are not confident of who we are in Christ, we will be operating from a sense of emptiness not strength. Without a healthy sense of self-worth which comes from seeing ourselves as God sees us and valuing ourselves as he does, we will not be free to serve in humility as Jesus did. Only when God has dealt with our sense of failure, low self-esteem and wrong view of ourselves can we forget about ourselves and reach out to serve others in his strength.[38]

Peter provides us with a clear example of this principle.

Immediately after this teaching of Jesus in the upper room, Peter tried ineffectively to serve Jesus with a sword in the Garden of Gethsemene. Then he denied his Lord in front of a servant girl. In both instances he was operating out of his emptiness, not fullness. Consequently, he felt defeated, discouraged and a total failure.

Before Jesus called Peter back into his service again, he first restored him through that loving encounter by the lake.[39] Peter had been called to be a 'fisher of men',[40] but had returned to what he knew best, fishing on the lake. Now he had failed at that too – they caught nothing all night. Following the miracle of catching a large haul of fish at Jesus' command, a hearty breakfast and an opportunity to reconfirm his love for Jesus, Peter was restored, renewed and called to follow his Master again. He was now ready for service. He was to change profession, from fisherman to shepherd. Jesus called him to the humble service of feeding his 'sheep' and 'lambs'.

'The first rule for biblical servanthood is to serve from a place of fullness, not emptiness.'[41] We need first to be forgiven, restored and filled with the love, power and resources that are available to us through Christ. This does not mean that we will always feel strong and confident. Often we are aware of our own inability, weakness and failures. But as Paul discovered, 'When I am weak, then I am strong', as God's power is made perfect in our weakness.[42] As Christ's servants, we are to draw constantly on his resources so that we are serving from a place of fullness and not emptiness.

Having looked at how Jesus modelled being a servant, we now turn to the example of the apostles. They had learned servanthood from him and provide further models for us.

CHRISTIANS AS SERVANTS/SLAVES OF CHRIST

Paul regarded himself as a servant or slave, which was a big step for someone who had once been a proud Pharisee. He starts three of his letters by introducing himself as the *doulos* (slave), which is actually translated in most versions as 'servant', of Jesus Christ or of God. Peter, James and Jude also refer to themselves as slaves.[43] It is interesting that James uses this word to describe his relationship to his half-brother Jesus – a very different view from the one he and his brothers had of Jesus originally.[44] The Apostle John identifies himself as God's slave and also refers to Moses as 'the slave of God'.[45] The figurative description of Christians as slaves of God or of Christ occurs over forty times in the New Testament.

Paul goes further. He identifies himself not only as a slave of Jesus Christ, but also of others: 'Although I am free and belong to no man, I make myself a slave *to everyone*, to win as many as possible'; and again, 'ourselves as your servants *(doulou* = slaves) for Jesus' sake'.[46] This was a logical consequence in Paul's thinking of being a slave of Jesus. He refers to his colleagues Epaphras and Tychicus as *sundouloi* or fellow-slaves in the Lord.[47] Being servants of Christ and of one another is the natural status for all Christians.

'So then,' says Paul, 'men ought to regard us as servants of Christ.'[48] Similarly, Peter urges us all to 'live as slaves (bondmen) to God'.[49] This concept of servanthood was something the apostles taught and practised. Not many Christians today would start their curriculum vitae by defining themselves as servants, let alone slaves. What a difference it would make if we all related to one another like that, in the family, in the church and in the world!

Slaves (*douloi*) of Christ

To our modern way of thinking the concept of slavery is totally abhorrent. A slave has been defined as 'someone whose person and service belong wholly to another'.[50] In the first century AD one person in three in Rome and one in five throughout the empire was a slave.[51] While some slaves were treated with respect and even given positions of authority, most were regarded as sub-human, their owners' property to treat or dispose of in any way they liked. It took another 1,800 years before the Christian conscience was sufficiently aroused to bring about the abolition of slavery, but still today, forms of slavery exist in some parts of the world.

So even the figurative use of the term 'slaves of Christ' to describe Christians can be discomforting and challenging to us. There are similarities and differences between these two types of slavery.

a) Human slavery is imposed by force, but Christians choose voluntarily to become slaves of Christ.

b) In both cases the owner had to pay a price for slaves, however Jesus did not pay in silver or gold but with his precious blood.[52]

c) Human slavery brings bondage, but slavery in Christ's service brings freedom, as the beautiful collect in *The Book of Common Prayer* expresses it: 'God . . . whose service is perfect freedom.'[53] This means a freedom to be what we were created to be, set free from slavery to self and sin.

d) Slaves to human masters do their work half-heartedly under duress or fear. Slaves of Christ serve out of a sense of love and joy.

The definition of slavery given above covers both states accurately. As Christ's purchased possession, the Christian is also someone whose person and service belong to Another. 'You are not your own; you were bought at a price. Therefore honour God with your body.'[54] Because of the incredible price paid to free me from slavery to sin, I voluntarily choose to become Christ's slave and seek to honour him.

The Freedom of Service

Another contrast between these two forms of slavery is that slavery to an earthly master means loss of freedom, whereas slavery to Christ brings freedom. In Romans 6 Paul explains how we were all slaves to sin, which leads to death (vv 6, 16), but that through his death on the cross Christ has set us free from the power of sin. We are not freed yet from the presence of sin or from temptation to sin, but we have now transferred our allegiance from sin to righteousness, from Satan to God. (vv 18, 22). Being a slave of Christ sets us free, not only from slavery to sin but from the fear of death.[55]

Paul takes the argument further in Galatians. He reminds us of our freedom, not to indulge in our sinful nature again, but to 'serve one another in love'.[56] This is how we demonstrate that we are serving God. Serving one another is a way of expressing our freedom in Christ. Peter picks up this theme too. He warns against false teachers who promise freedom by 'appealing to the lustful desires of human nature'. He says that this will lead to depravity, 'for a man is a slave to whatever has mastered him'.[57] We have the choice of being slaves to sin or slaves to righteousness. If we choose righteousness we are now free to serve God and one another. In 1520 Martin Luther wrote, 'A Christian man is a perfectly free man, lord of all, subject to none. A Christian man is a perfectly dutiful servant of all, subject to all.'[58]

How do we make this change from serving sin to serving God? How do we stop ourselves slipping back into previous forms of slavery? Clearly we cannot do this in our own strength. So God has provided us with his Holy Spirit to enable us to serve him as we should.

Serving in the Spirit

Serving sin is easy because it is second nature to us, but serving righteousness and serving others is hard. So God has provided us with the resources that we need to do this. In the days of human slavery, owners often branded their slaves with a seal or mark of ownership on their skin. Paul uses this metaphor to describe how God has 'set his seal of ownership on us, and put his Spirit in our hearts as a deposit, guaranteeing what is to come'.[59] This is the fulfilment of the prophecy of Joel: 'Even on my servants [slaves, *doulous*] both men and women, I will pour out my Spirit in those days, and they will prophesy.'[60]

In the same passage where Paul urges us to 'serve one another' we are told to 'live by the Spirit'.[61] 'To serve one another and to serve in the Spirit are inseparable concepts.'[62] We can only effectively serve others in love as we are empowered by the Spirit of God. Paul goes on to define the fruit of the Spirit which describes the character of those who live by the Spirit. The fruit of the Spirit, not the gifts of the Spirit, are the real evidence of a Spirit-filled life, and these are the qualities which should be seen in God's slave. They are the bench-mark against which we assess our service: 'The fruit of the Spirit is love, joy, peace, patience, kindness, goodness, faithfulness, gentleness and self-control.'[63] This leads us to explore further the kind of character God's servant should have.

THE CHARACTER OF THE SERVANT

Paul outlines to Timothy a brief profile of what the Lord's servant should be like:

The Lord's servant must not quarrel.
He must be kind towards all,
a good and patient teacher,
who is gentle as he corrects his opponents.[64]

Using this statement as a basic description of what 'the Lord's servant' should be like, we have first of all a picture of someone who is humble, even in his attitude towards his opponents.

Humility

Humility was not regarded as a virtue or a desirable quality by the prevailing Greek culture of the day, but the New Testament writers emphasised its importance. Peter said, 'Clothe yourselves with humility.'[65] He and the other disciples had seen humility as a hallmark of the life of Jesus – who had 'the very nature of a servant and . . . humbled himself.'[66] Jesus gave us a glimpse into his own character, when he said: 'Learn from me, for I am gentle and humble in heart.'[67] These two qualities are key indicators of whether we are becoming like our Master. Paul claimed that he 'served the Lord with great humility', and so urges us to 'be completely humble and gentle'.[68]

The humble person does not quarrel or act aggressively. There are times when it is appropriate to disagree or challenge something that is wrong, but that is different from quarrelling or being negative towards others. People tend to quarrel when their pride has been hurt, when they feel insecure or when they don't have a healthy sense of who they are. When we are secure in who we are in Christ there is no need to be quarrelsome. Instead of quarrelling, the servant should be a peacemaker, but we can only be peacemakers if we are at peace within ourselves.

Peacemaking

This is not usually the same thing as pacifying or just being passive. Sometimes making peace is hard work, and there is a cost to pay. When we actively intervene in a situation of strife we will probably be hurt and misunderstood. Our Lord 'made peace through the blood of his cross'.[69] Jesus said: 'Happy are those who work for peace; God will call them his children!'[70] He wants his servants to be peacemakers. The Church desperately needs peacemakers, and the world is crying out for those who know how to make peace. It takes more courage to make peace than to make war; to sow harmony than to spread discord.

Kindness

The Lord's servant is to be 'kind towards all'. This quality is expressed as much by our attitudes to people as by our actions for them. It is so easy to think critical and judgemental thoughts of others, even if we do not put them into words. Kind actions result from thinking kindly about others, assuming the best of them and having their interests at heart. Kindness is contagious and generally brings out the best in people. The servant who dispenses kindness is a powerful agent for good. Jesus said that kindness rebounds: 'Happy are those who are merciful to others; God will be merciful to them.'[71]

Patience

We live in a pressured world with so many demands on our time and energy that patience represents a real challenge for most of us. Everyone is in such a hurry, mostly preoccupied with their own concerns, often too busy to listen to others or to God and to notice the needs of those around them. Even people involved in a 'Christian ministry' can be consumed by busyness, which undermines the effectiveness of their service.

One of the things that stands out in the Gospels is the way Jesus never seemed in a hurry, even though he had such a great mission to complete in such a short time. He was patient with the crowds clamouring for his attention and patient with his disciples who were so slow to learn. Patience is listed as part of the fruit that the Holy Spirit wants to develop in us.[72]

Gentleness

In the context of this passage, Paul tells Timothy to be gentle in his teaching, especially with those who oppose him. Gentleness is not weakness, but controlled strength. We have already noted that Jesus said gentleness was part of his own character. Obviously, there were many other qualities of his character that he could have referred to, such as love or righteousness, but it would seem that God's Servant wants his servants to develop these two qualities in particular: humility and gentleness. What a difference this would make both in our fellowships and in the world if these were characteristic of our lifestyle.

One of Jesus' closest followers and friends described him as being 'full of grace and truth'.[73] Jesus came to earth to bring us God's truth, but it was his grace that drew men and women to him. This is the model for us his servants. We too need to be concerned with truth in a culture characterised by untruth and distorted values, but the extent to which our character displays his grace and gentleness determines the effectiveness of our service.

Faithfulness

In describing Epaphras and Tychicus, Paul emphasises their faithfulness.[74] Again he wrote: 'It is required in stewards, that a man be found faithful.'[75] This is a prime requirement of anyone who is a steward, manager or servant. In the parable of the talents, the servants who had been faithful were rewarded with their master's praise and greater privilege.[76] Some people have served God faithfully for many years without seeing much fruit or success. The Lord rewards our faithfulness in the way we serve him, rather than the degree of achievement we attain.

Light

Jesus said, 'You are the light of the world.'[77] This is one of the most powerful ways to be an effective servant. Charles Swindoll points out that the distinctive characteristics of light are that it is silent, gives direction and attracts attention to its source.[78] This is the goal of our service, not to serve in a showy, noisy way that attracts attention to ourselves, but in a manner which directs others to Christ.

THE NEXT LIFE

Christians are God's children,[79] but being also God's servants is something which bonds us closely to him. In an amazingly intimate conversation Jesus had with his disciples he tells them that he does not call them servants any longer but his friends.[80] Clearly, they were his servants as we always will be, but our relationship with Jesus transcends the normal boundary between master and servant. As followers of Christ we are all his brothers and sisters, disciples, servants and friends.

This relationship is not only for our lifetime on earth but for eternity. The Apostle John recorded a vision he was given of the future and in it we read: 'The throne of God and of the Lamb will be in the city, and his servants will serve/worship him. They will see his face, and his name will be on their foreheads.'[81] We do not know what kind of work he will give us to do, but we do know that if we have been faithful in our service here on earth, we will be trusted with greater responsibilities in the future.

Well done, good and faithful servant! You have been faithful with a few things; I will put you in charge of many things. Come and share your master's happiness![82]

SUMMARY

The concept of service is woven through the Bible from Genesis to Revelation and is something which unites human beings with their Creator. Jesus lived his life on earth as God's perfect Servant, providing us with the example to follow and the Holy Spirit to make it possible. The apostles taught that we should be servants of Christ and of one another. Servanthood is at the heart of life in the kingdom of God so, like Paul, let us learn to serve God with our whole heart.[83]

REFLECTIONS AND EXERCISES

1. WORK   What is your philosophy of work? Is your work
   ethic consistent with a biblical perspective? Does it include
   worship?
• Reflect on this in your journal, or discuss it together if you
   are part of a small group.

2. JESUS   How did Jesus model servanthood? Check through
   the references given under the section, 'Jesus, the Servant
   King' (notes 24–39) as a start to a study of Jesus the servant.
   If we get the pattern right it is easier to follow.
• Begin each day by praying, 'Lord Jesus, I would so
   appreciate it if you would bring me someone today whom I
   can serve.'[84]

3. SLAVES   The apostles defined themselves as 'slaves of Jesus
   Christ'. How does this title fit for you? Check out the
   references in the New Testament where the term slave
   (*doulos*) occurs, using *Young's Analytical Concordance*. It may
   surprise you, as in many of these instances the word
   'servant' is used in place of 'slave' in most translations.

4. CHARACTER   Who we are becoming in our character is
   the ultimate test of our service for God. Reflect on the
   development of humility, kindness, patience, gentleness and
   faithfulness in your life.
• It would be helpful to do this exercise in a small group with
   people who know one another well and can reflect back
   what they see in each other.

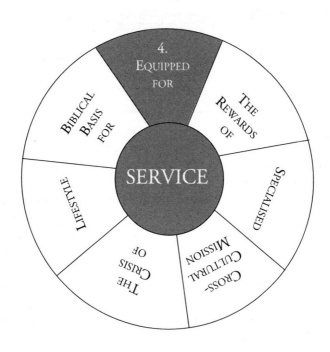

4.
EQUIPPED
FOR

THE
REWARDS
OF

BIBLICAL
BASIS
FOR

SPECIALISED

SERVICE

LIFESTYLE

THE
CRISIS
OF

CROSS-
CULTURAL
MISSION

Four

Equipped for Service

*'So that the person who serves God may be fully
qualified and equipped'*

Paul [1]

When God called Moses to serve him by leading the
Israelites out of Egypt, Moses complained that he didn't
have the ability or the eloquence for the task. God promised to
go with him, teach him what to say and be his strength and
companion. Then God asked him, 'What is that in your hand?'
All he had was a stick, so God said, 'Take this staff in your hand
so that you can perform miraculous signs with it.'[2]

We often complain that we do not have the ability or skills
to serve God effectively. He asks us the same question, '*What
do you have in your hand?*'[2] The best way to serve is to express
who we are through the outworking of our own unique
giftedness, character and training – to use just 'what we have'.
Anything else would be phoney.

Sometimes we may serve in response to an urgent situation,
and this is appropriate; we cannot turn our backs on a pressing
need before our eyes, just because we don't feel fully equipped
to meet it. When we respond to a need out of compassion, we
attempt to do something to help, even though we may not feel
competent. On the other hand, 'If I were to let my life be taken
over by what is urgent, I might very well never get around to

what is essential.'[3] Our service is more likely to be effective when we focus on the essential rather than the urgent. The important thing for a servant is to be equipped and ready for service.

This chapter looks at various aspects of our preparation and equipping for service.

MOTIVATION

Other-centred

In Chapter One we described the struggle we all have to move from being self-centred to becoming other-centred. We saw that it is not possible to be truly other-centred unless we have a healthy attitude towards ourselves, and good self-esteem. This means being able to see myself as God sees me: of great value to him, totally accepted and loved. There is a lot of misunderstanding, especially among Christians, about self-esteem.[4]

Jesus, Paul and James all summed up the basis of all relationships, and naturally of all service, in the statement: 'Love your neighbour as you love yourself.'[5] If you don't love, value and esteem yourself, you will not be able to love, value and esteem your neighbour properly. You cannot give away what you do not have. When you have a healthy attitude towards yourself, you can then forget about yourself and be fully available to love and serve your neighbour. It is then possible to 'consider others better than yourself', and be committed to their interests as well as your own.[6] A person who loves him/herself properly is free to move from being self-centred to becoming other-centred.

Christ-centred

Love for Jesus is the primary motivating force for Christian service. In two passages describing his service for God, Paul defined his driving force: 'For to me, to live is Christ', and 'Christ's love compels us'.[7] He was totally other-centred in his desire to reach anyone and everyone with the Good News, because he was Christ-centred. Being Christ-centred means that the driving force of our life and service is our love for him. The love of Christ must 'compel us', as it did Paul. It also means that Jesus becomes our model, and we will seek to learn from him how to go about our serving. We will want to be like him as servants.

In the last chapter, we saw how Peter was discouraged and defeated, and considered himself a failure as a servant after betraying his Lord. Jesus met him again after the resurrection and asked him one simple question: 'Do you love me?' In fact, he asked him three times to be quite sure.[8] The question was not: 'Do you want to serve me?', but 'Do you really love me?' The word for love Jesus used twice was *agapeö* – total, unconditional, giving love. Peter struggled to reply, and each time used the word *phileo*, meaning 'I am your friend'. However, he went on to prove his love for Christ with a lifetime of loyal service ending with a martyr's death. In the same way, our love for Jesus can be the driving force which provides the motivation we need to be his servants.

BALANCED LIVING

Wholeness

The effective servant is someone who is balanced and growing in all areas of life. Balanced people are able to care for the needs of others while at the same time nurturing their own wholeness and growth. Jesus provided a wonderful model of this. He took care of his *physical* health and had plenty of exercise by walking everywhere. When he was tired after a hard day's work he went to sleep in the boat, and didn't offer to take a turn with the rowing. After a long walk he sat and rested and enjoyed a cool drink.[9]

Jesus also took care of his *social* needs and spent quality time with his friends. He developed his *mind* and was able to counter the attempts of the best legal and theological brains of the day to trap him. The Gospel record shows he was comfortable in expressing all his *emotions* – love, anger, disappointment, joy, fear. Although fully divine, he became fully human and lived a balanced life. Above all, Jesus constantly nurtured his *spiritual* life and drew his strength from regular time with his Father. This is a lifestyle all servants should emulate.[10]

Boundaries

An important part of being an effective servant is to be able to recognise appropriate limits and set boundaries in our relationships. People with a servant heart sometimes find it difficult to say 'No' to any request for help. This is a sure way to move into overload and burnout, and so cease to be effective servants. People who lack boundaries in life can hurt others as well as themselves. Quite a lot has been written about the importance of having established boundaries and appropriate controls in our lives.[11] Defining clear boundaries and limits in our relationships is not being selfish but rather shows respect for ourselves as well as others.

God respects our boundaries. He does not force his will on us, and he wants us to make wise choices and take responsibility for our lives. Jesus loved everyone equally and was moved with compassion when confronted by need, but he did not respond to every demand for his presence and power. On one occasion when he had ministered successfully in Capernaum, the crowds returned the following morning wanting Jesus to continue teaching and healing, but he was nowhere to be seen. Peter eventually found him in a solitary place and said, 'Everyone is looking for you.' Jesus replied: 'Let us go somewhere else – to the nearby villages – so that I can preach there also.'[12]

When asked to perform miracles to prove his divinity, Jesus chose not to.[13] There are many examples of him saying 'No' when it was appropriate. If we are unable to say 'No' it means that the word 'yes' has become a knee-jerk reflex to us rather than a decision. I (John) have always found the word 'no' a difficult one. I realise as I look back on my childhood that I developed the habit of always saying 'Yes' to people because I really wanted them to like me. My self-esteem was based on their approval, not on a true awareness of who I was in God's eyes. It took some years to learn that my worth does not depend on what I do, but on who I am. People appreciate a genuine 'Yes' far more than a false one. Saying 'No' when it is appropriate is also appreciated and encourages others to be healthily assertive also.

OUR NATURAL GIFTING AND PERSONALITY

Recently we purchased a newer car with different features and peculiarities from those of our old vehicle. We considered it was to our advantage to study the manual, even though most of it was in a foreign language, and to find out all we could from people who understood the 'personality' of this make of car.

All of us have a unique mix of gifts, talents and skills. The trouble is that many people have not identified them fully and so haven't discovered yet who they are. If I do not understand my own personality, I am missing vital information that can help me to get the most out of life and become a more effective servant. More than that, I am in effect saying to God: 'I'm not really interested in the gifts you have given to me. I can't be bothered to find out what they are.'

93

PERSONALITY TESTS

For a number of years we have used psychological tests in our counselling in order to help people better understand themselves and others. Many personality profiles have been designed for a variety of purposes, and are often used to assess job applicants. Frequently, people who complete these tests for the benefit of their employers do not have the results explained to them, and consequently miss out on the benefit to themselves. We also conduct psychological assessments for candidates applying to various missionary societies. While this information is important to a mission board, we believe it's even more important that the candidate is made aware of it so their service will be more effective.

We have found the following tests most helpful in obtaining an overall picture of a person's personality, providing the results are discussed fully with the individual concerned. These profiles look at different aspects of a person's temperament. The two also overlap and provide a useful check on each other. Both have been used with many thousands of people, and have been thoroughly researched and evaluated.

1) The Myers-Briggs Type Indicator

This inventory was designed by Katharine Briggs and her daughter Isabel Myers soon after World War II. Their work was based on the personality theories of Swiss psychiatrist Carl Jung, by which he explained differences between healthy people.[14] Isabel Myers wrote the book *Gifts Differing* (a reference to Romans 12:6, AV) to explain the theory.[15] Much work and research has been done on this instrument since then to develop it into a useful tool.[16] Type theory is a way of explaining normal psychological behaviour without being judgemental.

Carl Jung observed that our active minds process information in two main ways, which he called: *perceiving* (sensing and intuiting) and *judging* (thinking and feeling). He also noticed that people are energised in two different ways: from the external world of people and activity, or from the internal world of ideas, feelings and memories. He called these two groups of people *extraverts* and *introverts*. It is through a combination of these eight basic elements or preferences that the MBTI profile is based. (See Figure 4:1.)

Preferences

We all use all of these functions but we are born with certain preferences, in the same way that we prefer to use our right or left hand for writing, although we have the use of both hands. For example, an introvert prefers introvert activities and is energised from within, but can also do extravert things. Sensing people rely primarily on their five senses (hearing, sight, touch, smell, taste) for information about the world around them, but can use their intuition as well. Intuiting people rely more on imagination and possibilities, though obviously they use their five senses as well. A thinking person comes to conclusions mainly through logical deduction and a feeling person in response to values and feelings, but both use the opposite process at times. Figure 4:2 shows the eight processes as four pairs of preferences and summarises their typical characteristics.

These descriptions of the eight preferences are generalised but give an overview. For different individuals some of these aspects are more significant than others. Your preferences are neither right nor wrong, they just 'are'. As we develop and mature we need to find a balance and become more comfortable with using our non-preference areas. It is helpful to discover our own preferences and tendencies in order to know ourselves, but it also helps in our relationships to be

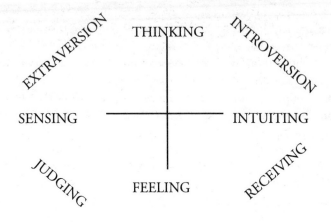

Fig. 4:1 Mental functions used in the MBTI Type Indicator

aware of how other people function. We all need each other and can benefit from one another's strengths, especially when working in a team.

Many times we have seen 'light bulbs come on' when couples have done this indicator together. They began to understand why some things have led to difficulties and misunderstandings between them in the past. It has not always been due to selfishness or stubbornness, but because they see and do things differently due to their different personalities. As they began to value and accept their own and each other's gifts, and to learn each other's 'language', these insights helped them to work together and build their relationship.[17]

Temperament and type

Four human temperaments were originally described by the physician Hippocrates (460–377 BC), viz., sanguine, choleric, phlegmatic and melancholic. However, these do not match up exactly with the four principle temperaments identified by Type theory: SJ, SP, NF, NT. The latter result from combining Intuition with the two judging functions (NF and NT); and Sensing with the two orientations to the outer world (SJ and SP). Within each of these four temperaments are four personality types, which are defined by four letters referring to the person's preferences. (See Figure 4:3.)

The combination of the four preferences in varying degrees leads to an infinite variety of personalities. It is beyond the purpose of this book to describe the temperaments or personality types in detail. However, those who have taken the indicator test are usually surprised by the accuracy of the descriptions that apply to themselves, and are rewarded by the insights this brings.

Type and work

The MBTI has been used to help people make career decisions and find the right profession or job for them. Some people move into a career because of the expectations and pressure of parents or others, but never find their work satisfying or reach their full potential. An understanding of one's gifts and natural abilities provides a sound basis for discovering how best to serve.[18]

Of course, many people have been able to serve effectively in situations and jobs that were not of their own choosing. However, when there is a choice, we will be better equipped to make the right decision if we know ourselves well. Christian servants trust God to guide them, but also need to learn to trust the gifts God has given them. Dag Hammerskjöld wrote in his book *Markings*: 'Don't be afraid of yourself. Live your individuality to the full – but for the good of others.'[19]

How we are energised:

(E) EXTRAVERSION vs	INTROVERSION (I)
Energised by people	Energised within/prefer solitude
Process externally/think aloud	Process internally/reflective
Active/out-going	Reserved/more quiet
Sociable/need interaction	Territorial/need space
See the breadth	See the depth

How we receive information:

(S) SENSING vs	INTUITING (N)
Facts and data important	Think more in ideas
Rely on their five senses	Rely more on their 'sixth sense'
Focus on details	See patterns and meanings
Practical	Imaginative
Live more in the present	Live a lot in the future
Can cope with repetition	Need variety and change

How we come to conclusions:

(T) THINKING vs	FEELING (F)
Objective/impersonal/cool	Subjective/personal/emotional
Operate from the head	Operate from the heart
Analyse things logically	Rely more on convictions/feelings
Quick to criticise	Quick to appreciate
Truth and justice important	Value harmony and relationships
Focus on principles	Focus on values

How we deal with the outside world:

(J) JUDGING vs	PERCEIVING (P)
Organised	Flexible/laid-back
Orderly/tidy	Disorganised/messy
Decisive/like closure	Find decisions hard/open-ended
Plan/sets goals well	More spontaneous
Strong work ethic	Well developed play ethic
Control important	Adaptable

Fig. 4:2 The Four Pairs of Preferences

I (John) found doing the MBTI most liberating. I discovered that my dominant function is 'F' (feeling) and that I have a strong preference for 'N' (intuition). However, I grew up in a 'big-boys-don't-cry' culture that denigrated feelings, and the message I received from church was that feelings were unreliable and suspect. Also, in the course of my medical training all the emphasis was on developing 'S' and 'T' abilities (sensing details and logical thinking) and I was taught to

		S		N	
		T	F	F	T
I	J	IS**T**J	I**SF**J	I**NF**J	I**NT**J
I	P	I**ST**P	I**SF**P	I**NF**P	I**NT**P
E	P	E**ST**P	E**SF**P	E**NF**P	E**NT**P
E	J	E**ST**J	E**SF**J	E**NF**J	E**NT**J

Fig. 4:3 Type Table of the Sixteen Personality Types
(The four temperaments are identified by bold underlined letters)

disregard my 'sixth sense' or 'gut feelings'. I needed, of course, to develop my 'non-preference' areas, but the impression I received as a young person was that my orientation to life was somehow wrong. I can now enjoy being who I really am.

I (Agnes) grew up in a culture which placed great emphasis on extraverted behaviour (E) and I tried to push myself to do extraverted things, such as public speaking and 'up front' activities. While I did learn to do some of these things, it was painful and did not really fit for me. I now realise since doing the MBTI that I am clearly an introvert (I) and can enjoy being who I am with gifts that are different. As an 'S', for example, I can complement John's 'N' and bring more substance to his visionary gifting and balance his optimism with realism!

The Keirsey Temperament Sorter

Another similar instrument was devised by David Keirsey which identifies the same personality types as the MBTI. We have found this to be a simple and effective test and have used it for many years. He expands and elaborates on the four temperaments, using the insights of other researchers such as Jung, Adler and Maslow.[20]

2) The Taylor-Johnson Temperament Analysis

This test was designed by Roswell Johnson in 1941 and has been developed and standardised by Robert Taylor and others over the years since.[21] It has been used extensively in both individual and marriage counselling. The test focuses on who I am *becoming* rather than what are my gifts. In this test, 'temperament' does not have the same meaning as in the MBTI, but refers to aspects of character and behaviour that a person is manifesting at the time. The questions are designed to identify nine different character traits, and the results place a person on a continuum in the following areas:

A. Nervous–Composed   **B.** Depressive–Light-hearted
C. Active-social–Quiet   **D.** Expressive-responsive – Inhibited
E. Sympathetic–Indifferent   **F.** Subjective–Objective
G. Dominant–Submissive   **H.** Hostile–Tolerant
I. Self-disciplined–Impulsive

When the test is analysed, the raw scores are converted into percentiles and then graphed. This places a person within a cohort of a hundred normal people of the same gender, which is more useful information than a plain score would be.

For example, if a person has a score of 40 in the 'Nervous–Composed' trait, this means there would be 39 people in the general population who would be more composed, and 60 people who are likely to be more nervous. The results are often quite revealing and may be surprising, and they help people to identify areas of their lives needing to be addressed, of which they may be unaware.

Patterns and change

Patterns emerge which can be helpful in understanding oneself. For example, an anxiety pattern consists of high scores in traits 'A', 'B' and 'F'. People with strong scores in 'C', 'D', 'E' and 'G' traits are probably good at relationships, whereas high scores on 'G' and 'H' suggest a person who is controlling and resentful or angry and likely to be poor at relating. A high score in 'B' and a low one in 'I' could indicate a sense of hopelessness and even alert the risk of suicide. A lot can be learned from exploring these test results with a counsellor. The results do not indicate a fixed description of a person, and negative patterns can be worked on and changed. A repeat test a year or so later could show that significant changes have been made.

SPIRITUAL GIFTING

It is clear from Scripture that God provides his servants with spiritual gifts enriching their natural gifts.[22] Examples of these gifts are enumerated in three places in particular in the New Testament: Romans 12:3–8, 1 Corinthians 12:4–11, 28 and Ephesians 4:7–13. We are told in each passage that the purpose of these gifts is to build up the Church, the 'body of Christ', and *'to prepare God's people for works of service'*.[23] There are several other gifts (*charismata*) mentioned in Scripture. In fact, our service for God is not going to be effective without using our spiritual gifts. For the most part, our spiritual gifts are an extension or anointing of our natural gifts.

Just as it is important to identify the natural gifts God has given us and develop them, so it is important to identify our spiritual gifts. Unfortunately, many Christians are not fully aware of their spiritual gifting, as these can be hard to evaluate objectively. Sometimes others can more easily recognise gifts in us and affirm them. Part of the responsibility of leaders in the church is to identify and acknowledge the spiritual gifts of the members of their congregation and provide opportunities for them to be used. If gifts are not clearly identified, people can be appointed to serve in the church in areas where they are not gifted. This leads to frustration for them and others, as well as resulting in ineffectual service.

For example, someone may be asked to teach a Sunday School class who has neither a natural teaching gift nor an affinity with young children. It is not likely to be edifying for the children and will certainly be discouraging for the teacher. A pastor may be appointed to a church where the expectation is that he or she will do most of the expository preaching. If the person's gift is in pastoral ministry and small group teaching, this mis-match would be to the detriment to both preaching and pastoral care in the church. At times we all may have to serve outside our area of gifting but, clearly, effective service is more likely to result when we are able to use our natural and spiritual gifts.

Spiritual Gifts (*charismata*)

The main spiritual gifts enumerated in Scripture are listed in Figure 4.4, but there are others. It is important for each of us to discover our spiritual gifts. The Apostle Peter tells us why: 'Each one should use whatever gift he has received *to serve others.*'[24] Our gifts are given in order to improve our ability to serve, and effective service will be limited if we are ignorant of our gifts. How then can we discover what our spiritual gifts are?

Sometimes spiritual people who know us well are able to identify our gifts more clearly than we can, and this is an important task of church leaders. At the same time, each one of us needs to ask God to show us clearly what spiritual gifts he has given us so that we can sharpen the focus of our service.

The Network Course

This programme was developed by Bill Hybels, Bruce Bugbee and associates at the Willow Creek Community Church, Chicago. They have produced a manual to help people identify their spiritual gifts, passion and personal style.[25] They define the 'servant profile' in three areas:

a) Your *passion* indicates WHERE you are best suited (what type of ministry). For example, your passion could be: reaching others for Christ; working with children or youth; teaching Scripture; discipling; caring for the aged.

b) Your *spiritual gifts* are WHAT you do best as you serve. They are in two groups: key gifts and supporting gifts. For example, a person's key gift might be mercy. She could also have supporting gifts accompanying mercy, such as encouragement, hospitality and shepherding.

1 Cor 12:8–10	1 Cor 12:28	Rom 12:6–8	Eph 4:11
Wisdom	Apostleship	Encouragement /Exhortation	Evangelism
Knowledge	Teaching	Giving	Pastor/ Shepherd
Faith	Helps	Leadership	
Healing	Administration	Mercy	

Miracle working	Other gifts (*charismata*) mentioned	
Prophecy	Hospitality	1 Peter 4:9
Discernment	Suffering	Philippians 1:29
Tongues	Marriage/singleness	1 Corinthians 7:7
Interpreting of tongues	Eternal life	Romans 5:15,16; 6:23
	Deliverance	Acts 27:14; 2 Corinthians 1:10–11

SUMMARY OF GIFTS: 'Speaking' and 'Serving'   1 Peter 4:11

Fig. 4:4. Spiritual Gifts Mentioned in the New Testament

c) Your *personal style* indicates HOW you serve. This is determined by a combination of how you are energised (either by people or tasks), and how you are organised (structured or unstructured). People fall into four categories, in varying degrees:

task oriented/structured   task oriented/unstructured;
people energised/structured   people energised/unstructured.

The manual provides a series of questions to answer in order to identify these three areas. This is then checked out and confirmed by those who know you, as well as through an opportunity to talk with a consultant experienced in administering the test.

A large number of people from our own church congregation have done the *Network* course, and have identified their spiritual gifts. This has helped them significantly to be able to serve within their gifting and not outside it, both in the church and the wider community. Recognising one another's gifts and affirming them has strengthened our fellowship. Many have found direction for gifts that were under-utilised, and some have offered since to do tasks within the church without waiting to be asked. It has resulted in a greater desire in many to be more involved and to work together.

Once we have identified our spiritual gifts we have a responsibility to use them in the service of the Master. Paul wrote to Timothy, 'Do not neglect the gift that is within you'.[26] God has not given us natural or spiritual gifts to be neglected and unused. Jesus spoke of the danger of doing this in his parable of the talents. He condemned the 'wicked, lazy servant' for burying in the ground the one talent that the master had given him.[27] On the other hand, there is also the danger of being proud of our gifts and using them for our own glory, not God's. John Bunyan warns that 'gifts are dangerous things, not in themselves, but because of those evils of pride and vainglory that attend them'.[28]

FUEL FOR SERVICE

Serving is hard work and drains our energy and resources, which constantly need to be replenished. Failure to do so leads at the least to a loss of our cutting edge as servants, and at worst to burnout or experiencing physical, emotional and spiritual exhaustion. We have counselled many Christian workers and missionaries who were in a state of burnout, or close to it. The causes of burnout are numerous and they tend to be cumulative and interact with one another. Sometimes people have been serving in situations where the pressures and stressors are great and they have had little support. However, it is also possible to move into burnout as a result of poor self-care. One of the quickest ways to burnout is to try to serve in your own strength – 'running your engine on the wrong oil'. Burnout is a preventable condition, and God does not intend us to live that way. Unfortunately, there is a myth abroad which infers that unless you have burnt out, you can't have been working hard enough![29] There are several ways that we can nurture ourselves and be nourished by God and others in order to improve our effectiveness as servants.

Nurture your Body

If my body truly is the 'temple of the Holy Spirit',[30] then it's my responsibility to take care of it and nourish it. Every machine requires maintenance, even one as efficient as the human body. We can do this in a number of simple and obvious ways:

- understand the principles of good nutrition and eat a healthy diet
- have adequate aerobic exercise on a regular basis each week
- ensure that we obtain enough rest and sleep
- aim to have one day off a week, as God intended
- plan times for recreation, perhaps a creative hobby.

Nurture your Soul

We have seen that Jesus maintained wholeness and cared for his body. The Gospel record shows us that, above all, Jesus nurtured his spiritual life and drew on his relationship with his Father. He said, 'I do nothing of my own but speak just what the Father has taught me.'[31] We have identified in this chapter some of the gifts and talents that we have been given for service. But our tools are ineffective on their own. It is only when we recognise our weakness and draw on the Lord's strength that we will be effective servants. Paul discovered that God's power was made perfect in his weakness, and 'when I am weak, then I am strong'.[32] Here are some of the main ways that we can draw on God's strength:

a) *The Scriptures.* Scripture is given 'so that the person who serves God may be fully *qualified and equipped* to do every kind of good deed'.[33] To have our minds and hearts saturated with the word of God is the best preparation for service. David wrote, 'I am but a pilgrim here on earth: how I need a map – and your commands are my chart and guide. I long for your instructions more than I can tell.'[34]

b) *Solitude.* The word of God needs to be internalised and to move from our heads to our hearts. This requires time for meditation, which is something that is missing from the lives of busy people. Meditation is the process of pondering on, delighting in and feeding on God's word, but is almost a lost art today. In the Scriptures we are encouraged to meditate on the law 'day and night'.[35] The psalmist claimed, 'I have more insight than my teachers', as a result of meditation on God's word.[36] This is not unrealistic even in a hectic lifestyle, because in actual fact we all spend a lot of time in short periods on our own during even a busy day.

The practice of setting aside regular times of solitude is essential for our spiritual nourishment. Jesus modelled this in his ministry and was prepared to rise early in the morning for it, or have time alone at the end of a day's work.[37] Introverts find solitude a little easier than extraverts, but for all of us making time for solitude requires determination and discipline.

However, it brings great rewards and our service will be all the poorer without it. Henri Nouwen describes solitude as 'that holy place where ministry and spirituality embrace'.[38]

c) *Prayer.* The art of prayer has to be learned. We can learn how to pray from books[39] and from the experience of others, but mainly through constant practice. The more we personally discover about prayer the more we are aware of our limitations as pray-ers. Prayer is co-operating with God in what he is doing in this world, in our lives and in the lives of others. The disciples asked the Lord to teach them to pray.[40] We too can learn much from Jesus: observing the way he modelled a life of prayer, from his teaching about prayer, and from studying his prayers recorded in the Gospels. If Jesus needed to pray, how much more do we in our service for him.

d) *The Holy Spirit.* It is the Holy Spirit who produces the character of a servant within us, such as Jesus displayed. Only as we are filled by the Spirit are we able to serve Christ effectively. This filling is not a one-off experience, but a continual infilling with the power of the Spirit. When Paul wrote: 'Be filled by the Spirit', he used the present continuous tense – in other words, '*be being* filled by the Spirit'.[41] If this is our daily experience, our service will then be the natural outworking of our relationship with Christ. It is significant that the prime qualification for people chosen to serve in the early church, even in menial tasks, was that they were 'known to be full of the Holy Spirit and wisdom'.[42] This phrase is repeated several times in the Acts of the Apostles, describing the way the early disciples lived.[43]

Even more significantly, Luke tells us that Jesus was full of and lived by the power of the Holy Spirit. He was led by the Spirit, filled with joy by the Spirit, ministered, taught and healed through the power of the Spirit.[44] Jesus endured the cross and was raised from the dead through the power of the Holy Spirit.[45] There was no aspect of his life and ministry that was not governed by the Holy Spirit. Where else can we find our source of strength and life to be his effective servants?

Another important part of our fuel for service is fellowship with other servants.

THE COMMUNION OF SERVANTS

We are not called to serve in isolation, and as servants of Christ we can encourage others and be encouraged by one another in our service. There is no place in God's kingdom for the individualist who operates on his own and not in fellowship or co-operation with other servants. We need each other. Effective work for God, whether at home or on the mission field, is done by teams who combine their gifts and talents. The principle of *synergy* comes into operation, where the resultant effect is more than the sum of the separate parts. Apart from organised teams, there is tremendous value in small support groups for the purpose of encouraging and strengthening one another as well as providing opportunity for challenge and growth.

a) 'Buddy' system
By this we mean two friends who agree to meet regularly to listen to and support one another, challenge each other, be accountable to one another, pray together and be a catalyst for each other's growth. This can be a great help to God's servants working in relatively isolated situations. It is also a valuable experience for those who may be in contact with many Christians but may not have an in-depth relationship with anyone. We have both found this practice invaluable for many years, and each meet at regular intervals for breakfast, lunch or coffee with one or more people for this purpose.

b) Supervision

A 'buddy' system is an informal arrangement, whereas supervision is more structured. A supervisor does not tell you what to do but is there to look (vision) over (super) your work and life. Every person who works with people, such as a pastor, counsellor or social worker should have supervision, not only to improve the efficiency of their work but also help them maintain a healthy lifestyle. It is so easy for busy 'people workers' to lose their focus, become unbalanced or even move into burnout. Sometimes it requires the objectivity of another to help us detect the occasions when our work with people gets mixed up in unhelpful ways with what is happening in our own lives (known technically as transference and counter-transference).

In our own counselling and spiritual direction work we have always received supervision at least monthly. We would not be without it. I (John) have trained as a supervisor and work in this capacity with a number of counsellors, social workers, pastors and people in other church ministries. I consider that I learn as much in these sessions as hopefully they do.

c) Spiritual Direction

This is a discipline that has been kept alive in the traditional churches down through the centuries, but has recently become more common among people from other denominations. The term is a little misleading, in that a spiritual director does not 'direct' a person's life, but walks with them from time to time on their spiritual journey. The spiritual director helps you discover what God may be saying to you in the current circumstances of your life, and challenges you about your walk with God or your prayer life. As Henri Nouwen puts it: 'Spiritual direction is direction offered in the prayer life of the individual Christian. It is an art which includes helping to discover the movements of the Holy Spirit in our life.'[46] We ourselves both benefit immensely through having regular spiritual direction, and I (Agnes) have trained as a spiritual director.

d) Groups

There are many kinds of groups that will promote growth. Some are directed towards spiritual development, such as church home groups and Bible studies. Other groups are aimed at more general growth, especially emotionally and socially. We have been part of such groups as participants or leaders for many years, and have gained so much from them.

Currently we are both involved in *Renovaré* groups, one for men and the other for women. Renovaré (renewal) groups were developed by Richard Foster, who together with James Smith produced a manual on how to run them: *A Spiritual Formation Workbook*.[47] The purpose of the Renovaré process is to encourage our development in the five major streams of Christian tradition. These are: the contemplative, charismatic, holiness, evangelical/evangelistic/biblical, and social action aspects of Christian life. Many Christians are relatively well developed in one or two of these aspects of their faith, but may have neglected others. A healthy servant is a balanced Christian.

Each group is comprised of three to five people, who meet regularly to encourage and challenge each other in these areas and to be accountable to one another. We find that every two weeks is ideal spacing, and we meet for an hour and a half. The session has a simple format and structure, and members of the group take turns to lead. Each time, the five areas are addressed by each person present, sharing something of their own experience, struggles and growth since they last met.

At the end of the time each member of the group identifies one specific discipline or aspect of growth to work on and then reports back next time. Everything shared, both joys and struggles, is kept confidential within the group. This builds the trust which is essential to enable people to be honest with one another.

True service is hard work and can be discouraging. We do need both the power of the Holy Spirit in our lives and also the encouragement of fellow servants to maintain our edge and freshness. The suggestions we have made here may not all apply to everyone, but some form of support is essential because we are very limited on our own.

SPECIFIC TRAINING

Identifying our natural and spiritual gifts is a good start, but these also have to be trained and developed. Many people take up a profession or receive some training before they clearly identify their gifts. Even so, identifying our gifts more precisely later in life will still enhance our skills. God can use any training we may have had in the work of his kingdom; but for whatever service we may be led into in the future there will always be need for further learning and training. We are never too old to learn. To stop learning is to stop living.

We may be tempted to think that anyone can serve and that it does not require training. On the contrary, to be an effective servant requires training at all levels of our person, as we have endeavoured to show in this chapter. We conclude with a powerful statement by Henri Nouwen: 'Training for service is not training to become rich but to become voluntarily poor; not to fulfil ourselves but to empty ourselves; not to conquer God but to surrender to his saving power.'[48]

SUMMARY

There are no short cuts to being an effective servant. God provides us all with natural and spiritual gifts for the task, but these have to be identified and developed. God's perfect Servant has modelled the kind of character that we need as servants, and the Holy Spirit is available to us just as he was to Jesus for his ministry. We also need to nurture our physical bodies and our relationships in order to maintain our effectiveness as servants.

REFLECTIONS AND EXERCISES

1. MOTIVATION   What motivates you for service? There are three alternatives, often in combination: Self-centredness, other-centredness, Christ-centredness.
- Explore the elements of your motivation in a small group, or on paper in your journal.

2. BALANCE   How balanced are you in all aspects of your life?   Have you set appropriate 'boundaries' in your service and relationships?
- When did you last say 'No' to a request, because it did not fit in with what you believe is God's plan for you? If you have difficulty with the word 'no', why do you think this is?

3. YOUR GIFTING   God has given you specific natural and spiritual gifts. Do you know clearly what these are? If you have not explored these already, consider taking one of the personality tests, such as MBTI, and also doing the *Network* course.
- This would be especially helpful for married couples and for people working in teams, to take these tests together in order to discover each other's strengths and improve their understanding and acceptance of one another.

4. NURTURE   Read through the sections again about nurturing your body and your soul. Are there any aspects of this which you are missing?
- Choose one physical nurturing activity and one of those aimed at nurturing your soul to start building into your life.

5. SUPPORT   Are there any suggestions from the section 'communion of servants' which would assist you in your ministry?

- Consider working with a 'buddy' for support and encouragement.
- How could a supervisor or spiritual director be of help to you right now?
- Explore the possibility of joining with a few friends in forming a small growth group.

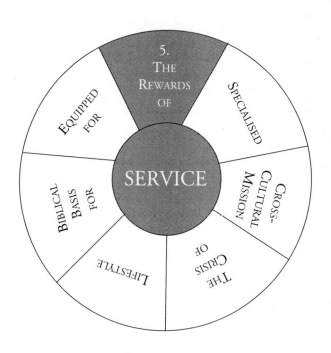

5. THE REWARDS OF SERVICE

SPECIALISED

CROSS-CULTURAL MISSION

THE CRISIS OF

LIFESTYLE

BIBLICAL BASIS FOR

EQUIPPED FOR

SERVICE

Five

Rewards of Service

'The reward of a thing rightly done is to have it done.'
                                                    Seneca[1]

One day a little mouse was playing in the woods. All at once she came upon a lion who was fast asleep and in her panic ran right across the lion's nose. The lion woke up and was about to kill her.

'Please don't kill me,' cried the mouse, 'let me go and some day I'll help you.'

'How could you possibly help me?' the lion said. He thought this was a big joke, but felt sorry for the mouse and decided to let her go.

Not long after this, the same lion was walking through the woods where a trap had been set to catch him. The lion was caught in a net made of ropes and couldn't get away. The little mouse heard him roar, went to see what was the matter and found the big lion unable to escape.

'You laughed at me,' said the mouse, 'when I told you one day I would help you, but you were kind to me and let me go then when you could have killed me. Now I'll help you to get out of the net.'

The little mouse gnawed at the ropes with her sharp teeth, and soon the lion was free.[2]

We may smile at this ancient Greek fable, but it illustrates the principle of rewards for service and kindness. Everything we do has consequences, including our service for God and others. The kind of service we have described so far in this book is clearly not done in order to receive a reward. True motivation for Christian service is love for God, desire to do his will and a compassion which reaches out to minister to those in need. This is summed up beautifully in the prayer of St Ignatius:

> Teach us good Lord to serve thee as thou deservest,
> To give and not to count the cost,
> To fight and not to heed the wounds,
> To toil and not to seek for rest,
> To labour and not to ask for any reward
>   save that of knowing that we do thy will.[3]

Jesus reminds us: 'When you have done everything you were told to do, say, "We are unworthy servants; we have only done our duty." '[4] As his servants, we do not expect or demand a reward; however, God is no one's debtor and we cannot out-give him. In fact, he loves to reward his children. In this chapter we look at some of the ways God chooses to reward us for our allegiance to him and our service for him.

OUR ULTIMATE REWARD

When God called Abraham to follow him, he made a covenant with him and said: 'Do not be afraid, Abram, I am your shield, your very great reward.'[5] The reward God promised for following him was not riches, or power, or long life, but *himself* – 'I am your reward.' Abraham went on to know God in a way that few others have done since; he was known as God's friend.[6] God once discussed his plans with him and he was even able to bargain with God.[7] It was Abraham's *faith*, not his works that God rewarded. We read, 'Abraham believed God, and it was credited to him as righteousness.'[8]

The amazing truth is that the same offer is open to us: 'Without faith it is impossible to please God, because anyone who comes to him must believe that he exists and that *he rewards those who diligently seek him*.'[9] As we seek God in faith he will reward us with the gift of himself. We too can have a relationship with him and access into his presence whenever we wish. God is our ultimate reward, and we can enjoy him now and for eternity. There are, however, also other rewards that God gives for service. The following are some of them.

HEALTH

Over recent years there has been some interesting research which indicates that being altruistic is good for your health, that people who reach out to help others tend to be healthier and live longer. 'Scientists have long noted an association between social relationships and health. More socially isolated or less socially integrated individuals are less healthy, psychologically and physically, and more likely to die.'[10] Reviews of a number of studies in this area show with remarkable consistency that social relationships influence life expectancy for both men and women. Being married is more beneficial to health, and becoming widowed detrimental, especially for men. Women's health seems to benefit much more than men from good relationships with friends and relatives.

The exact mechanism of the benefit of social interaction is not fully established. However, it is known that the presence of another person, and especially physical contact, modulates human cardiovascular activity and reactivity in general, particularly in stressful contexts.[11] The social contact and support provided is not only of benefit to the health of the recipients but also to that of the care-givers.

Helper's Calm

An analysis of the experience of several thousand women who regularly help others has shown interesting results.[12] Most of them experience what is now called 'helper's calm', which is due to the release of endorphins in the brain and is similar to 'runner's high'. These endorphins (natural opiates) produce good feelings that arise during social contact with others. According to Harvard cardiologist, Dr Herbert Benson, altruism works through the relaxation response which reverses the body's stress response. For example, subjects interviewed reported loss of stress-related disorders such as headaches.

Helper's calm, or pleasure from altruism, doesn't arise from caring at a distance, such as donating money to charity, but requires personal contact with those being helped. While this good feeling is most intense when actually touching or listening to someone, it can also be recalled later when reflecting on the experience (remembered wellness). It was also found that the health benefits of helping others only seem to be present when the help is offered voluntarily.

PLEASURE AND SATISFACTION

We have just described the physiological pleasure (helper's calm) resulting from altruistic service, and the health benefits that this brings. However, pleasure from service and giving to others goes much further than that. Jesus said, 'It is more blessed to give than to receive' or 'There is more happiness in giving than in receiving' as The Good News Bible translates it.[13] The Greek word *makarios*, translated 'blessed' in many versions, means fortunate, happy or well off. William Barclay states that '*makarios* describes that joy which has its secret within itself, which is serene, untouchable and self-contained; that joy which is completely independent of all the chances and changes of life.'[14] It is a joy that is deeper than happiness, which so often depends on what 'happens' to us. While we all derive pleasure from receiving good things in life, Jesus assures us that the pleasure from giving is even greater.

Whether or not we receive back as much as we give is not important. One return that giving always brings is *joy* to the giver. Paul J. Meyer is a highly successful businessman who has made giving his lifestyle. He describes his experience this way: 'I don't give to be paid back, I give because I need to give. I feel almost selfish. If I could, I'd give every minute of the day. That's the thrill of giving.'[15]

Many can testify to the immense pleasure they have received from offering hospitality to strangers, giving to those in need, or alleviating sickness, hunger, illiteracy or poverty, especially for those who are unable to repay. We can certainly say that the years we spent serving the people living in the jungles of Papua New Guinea were among the happiest years of our life. Part of the joy and pleasure was from the fact that our income did not come from those we served, as we were totally supported by New Zealand churches. Pleasure can be a transient experience and although some service may be hard work without much pleasure, it can still be satisfying and rewarding.

Satisfaction

Satisfaction and pleasure are similar feelings, but may or may not occur together. Satisfaction results from a job well done or a goal accomplished. We and our medical team received great satisfaction from seeing the health of the local tribespeople in PNG (Papua New Guinea) improve significantly. In eleven years, the infant mortality was more than halved. Life-tables prepared from our medical records showed that the life expectancy of adults had increased by about ten years over that period.

This was the result of a lot of hard work, not only in the hospital but through regular visits to many villages for medical surveys and monthly infant welfare clinics. Most of this was done on foot, sometimes riding horseback or using mountain motorbikes, climbing mountain tracks and crossing rivers. I (John) estimate that I walked at least 4,000 miles on medical patrols collecting the data on which our life tables were based. It was also rewarding to leave behind trained medical personnel to carry on the work, and then to return twenty-five years later to find some of them still actively engaged in caring for others. Satisfaction is a legitimate reward for service.

In Chapter Six, we record comments from a number of people we interviewed about the rewards they experienced from their various types of service.

PERSONAL DEVELOPMENT

Biological Basis for Altruism

Research on childhood behaviour points to the conclusion that we are all born with a tendency to altruism, or prosocial behaviour as it is sometimes called.[16] For example, babies of about a year old will often look upset when someone falls down or cries. Even newborns cry more intensely at the sound of another child crying than in response to other equally loud noises. Toddlers will try to comfort other children in a rudimentary way, such as patting the head of someone who seems to be in pain. When one of our daughters first went to school, she used to burst into tears if another child in the class was being reprimanded or was upset.

While there may be a biological basis for altruism, we live in a society where looking after 'Number One' is the norm. Human beings have a strong bias towards selfishness. Both tendencies are reflected in our community. Appeals for funds to help those who have suffered disaster or tragedy are often followed by an amazing response. Individual acts of bravery in caring for others are reported in the news quite frequently. Conversely, we also know that people can be callously indifferent towards others in need. The twentieth century saw brutality and genocide on a massive scale in many countries in the world.

Social Factors

There are a number of factors that have a bearing on this phenomenon. For example, it has often been observed that people living in smaller communities tend to be more concerned about caring for others around them. In contrast, it is a feature of urban life that people respond to the added pressures and stress in the city by reducing their involvement with others. Sometimes people can live in adjacent apartments or houses for years without being aware of the circumstances or even the names of their neighbours. We are apt to respond more caringly to people we know, or to those with whom we can identify, than we do to strangers or people outside of our culture.

It is possible that the immediacy of television, which brings the reality of a disaster happening thousands of miles away right into our living rooms, also dulls our sensitivity. We can be overwhelmed by the enormity of the problem and our inadequacy to do much about it, and so become hardened as we are exposed almost daily to human suffering.

Prosocial behaviour is not always altruistic. Sometimes we may respond to another's need out of a sense of guilt or to relieve our own discomfort. The eleventh-century philosopher, Thomas Hobbes, claimed that people always act out of self-interest.[17] On one occasion he was seen giving money to a beggar. When asked why, he explained that he was mostly trying to relieve his own distress at seeing the beggar's distress!

Many of us have probably had a similar feeling at times, especially when travelling in Third World countries; but this is not the whole story.

Psychological and Spiritual Maturity

The degree of other-centredness that we display is related to our psychological and spiritual maturity. Whether we become selfish, or are other-centred, depends largely on our training and our value system. We all are familiar with this struggle. The good news is that we can change and grow. We can develop a servant attitude to life.

Studies which carefully observed the behaviour of children at play found that youngsters who shared their toys or lollies with others had a lower need for approval than those who did not share. The principle this illustrates is that if we feel good about ourselves, we are more likely to respond to the needs of others. Mature people who have a healthy sense of self-worth are not preoccupied with their own pain. Consequently, they can more easily forget about themselves and reach out to serve others.

This is the same principle that was defined in Chapter Three about serving out of fullness not emptiness. If we know who we are and are comfortable with the way God has made us, we are free to focus on the needs of others. Jesus summed it up in the well-known words, 'Love your neighbour as yourself.'[18] This is ultimately rewarding.

Being other-centred is not easy. It results from emotional and spiritual growth. Neither of these will happen automatically, but need to be desired and worked for. Christians learn to draw on God's strength daily in order to develop qualities of kindness, unselfishness and unconditional love. However, this growth in maturity does not merely result in our individual development but has rewards and benefits in our community life.

COMMUNITY DEVELOPMENT

Personal Relationships

The whole emphasis of the Bible is on community and relationships: how to make a good relationship with God and with others. The two go together. In fact, it is not possible to say we love God unless we love others.[19] The reality of our Christian faith is demonstrated by the quality of our relationships. In Chapter Two we described how the principle of service impacts all our relationships: friendships, marriage, parenting, grandparenting and reaching out to others. If we see our social contacts as opportunities for service, this not only transforms our service but strengthens our relationships.

The Church Community

Some people have had a negative experience of church life. However, the church is still the vehicle God has chosen to bring healing to a broken world. Paul frequently used the metaphor of the body to describe the Church of Jesus Christ. For example:

> Just as there are many parts to our bodies, so it is with Christ's body. We are all parts of it, and it takes every one of us to make it complete, for we *each have different work to do.* So we belong to each other, and each needs all the others.[20]

In Chapter One, we thought about how all members of the body must work together for there to be harmony and effectiveness. We must work together not only for efficiency but also in order to build one another up in Christ. This actually happens as we serve one another in love. The church

125

community becomes whole when we serve Christ by serving one another. Then we can effectively reach out to the world, because only when the church community is strong and whole will it be able to fulfil the great commission given by Christ.

The Wider Community

The church is intended to be a working model of God's plan for the world. Just as salt has a preserving influence when it permeates food, so the members of Christ's body can spread his love through serving a broken world. In the same way that a small amount of yeast will spread through a lump of dough and cause it to rise, so a 'servant community' can influence and change a 'selfish community'. Jesus used both these metaphors to describe the working of his kingdom.[21]

Richard Foster writes: 'True service builds community. It quietly and unpretentiously goes about caring for the needs of others. It puts no one under obligation to return the service. It draws, binds, heals, builds. The result is the unity of the community.'[22]

THE REWARD OF FRUIT

The Lord looks for fruit in our lives: 'This is to my Father's glory, that you bear much fruit, showing yourselves to be my disciples.'[23] Fruitfulness is evidence of spiritual life, but it does not result from our own efforts. It is produced as we 'remain in the vine', vitally connected to Jesus, who said: 'Apart from me you can do nothing.'[24] Spiritual fruit is manifested in three ways:

a) The primary fruit God looks for in his servants is 'the *fruit of the Spirit*: love, joy, peace, patience, kindness, goodness, faithfulness, gentleness and self-control.'[25]
b) Paul prayed that Christians would 'live a life worthy of the

Lord and may please him in every way: bearing fruit in *every good work.*'[26] Doing good does not make us more spiritual, but true spiritual life results in good works.

c) Then there is the *fruit of our witness*, expressed in the lives of people we lead to Christ or build up in their faith.

There is nothing more rewarding than seeing people coming into the kingdom of God as a result of our service for him, however small a part we may have played in the process. As a doctor and midwife, we have both assisted in the birth of hundreds of babies. We never ceased to be excited, along with the parents, as we shared the joy that always accompanies the miracle of new life. Similarly, there is great joy in being a 'spiritual midwife', assisting in the miracle of 'the new birth', when someone comes into the reality of salvation in Christ. Jesus told us that this joy is also felt in heaven itself.[27]

Paul referred to their converts in Thessalonica, who were the fruit of their labours, as: 'our joy, or the crown in which we will glory in the presence of our Lord Jesus Christ when he comes . . . indeed, you are our glory and joy'.[28] Michael Griffiths, a missionary statesman has written, 'The cross-cultural missionary has the most satisfying work in the world and the most lasting – the planting of churches, which may last for hundreds of years. The missionary has enormous satisfaction of leading people to faith in Christ, and making friends for life.'[29]

Jesus warned us against getting too carried away by seeing fruit for our labours. He once sent out seventy-two of his disciples on a mission to prepare the way for his forthcoming visit to a number of towns. They returned very excited about their success. In the debriefing session that followed, Jesus said, 'Do not rejoice that the spirits submit to you, but rejoice that your names are written in heaven.'[30] He wasn't discouraging them for being excited at seeing God at work against the forces of evil – as the same passage states how full of joy he was – Jesus was encouraging them (and us) to put it into perspective. God is the one who produces spiritual results, and we should never lose sight of the wonder that we have been brought into his kingdom and are able to serve him.

Service Without Apparent Fruit

It is a fact of life that some of the Lord's servants have worked for him faithfully for many years in situations where there is little apparent 'fruit' to show for all their service. They cannot point to many people, perhaps not even one, who came into the kingdom as a result of their work. Many of us have had the experience of praying for years for someone, perhaps a family member, whom we have not seen come to faith. We have not seen the fruit of our prayers. God has not promised that we will see the fruit of our service for him or our prayers in this life; only eternity will provide the final evaluation of our service. It is significant that the heroes of faith listed in Hebrews chapter 11 were identified as heroes because of their faith, despite the fact that 'they *did not receive* the things promised' in their lifetime.[31]

Sometimes we may work hard to sow the seed and other servants reap the harvest, then at other times it may be the reverse. This is part of God's plan. He is the one at work in this world and his servants work with him. Paul addresses this issue clearly: 'Neither he who plants nor he who waters is anything, but only God, who makes things grow. The man who plants and the man who waters have one purpose, and *each will be rewarded* according to his own labour. For we are God's fellow-workers.'[32]

From a human perspective, the mission of Jesus could have been described initially as a failure. He was born into a humble home, in an insignificant village in a backwater of the Roman

Empire. He spent most of his life as the village carpenter, then three years as an itinerant teacher and healer. He drew together a small band of followers, a devoted but poorly educated lot who had no standing in the community. At his crucifixion, when Jesus needed them most, they deserted him. After the resurrection they rejoiced to see him again, but were directionless and powerless until they were transformed by the power of the Holy Spirit. Two millennia later, however, the message of Jesus is still impacting lives around the world and many millions of people have found eternal life in him.

A man once went to bring the gospel to a tribe who had never heard of Jesus. He struggled for three years to try and learn the language and to cope with the great difficulties of the situation, but was unsuccessful. Eventually, his health gave way and he reluctantly left without seeing any obvious fruit for his work. A few years later, a linguist went to live with these people, learned their language and translated the New Testament. As he told them about Jesus, the people said, 'We've already met him. In fact, he lived with us for three years, and we are so glad to know more about him.' As a result, many of their number became committed Christians.

The rewards of service for God now are many, but sometimes we are unable to recognise them. The Bible assures us that God will also reward his servants in the future.

FUTURE REWARDS

Jesus said: 'Behold I am coming soon! My reward is with me, and I will give to everyone according to what he has done.'[33] The Greek word *misthos* (translated 'reward') literally means wages or payment for work done. As this verse implies, our reward will be measured in proportion to what we have done, whether good or bad. The word *misthos* is also used in the general sense of reward, as when Jesus said of his servants who had experienced persecution, 'Rejoice and be glad, because great is your reward in heaven.'[34]

When Will This Take Place?

Paul wrote: 'We must all appear before the judgment seat of Christ, that each one may receive what is due to him for the things done while in the body, whether good or bad.'[35] This judgment seat (Greek *bëma*) is referred to twice in the New Testament, and is not the same as the judgement throne of Christ, which separates the saved and the lost, the 'sheep' and the 'goats'.[36] 'At this *bëma*, believers are to be made manifest . . . there they will receive rewards for their faithfulness to the Lord.'[37] Paul tells us that the quality of each person's work will be tested by fire. 'If what he has built survives, he will receive his reward. If it is burned up, he will suffer loss; he himself will be saved, but only as one escaping through the flames'[38]

The concept of a differentiation in rewards for service done must be balanced by the clear teaching of Scripture that 'all of God's children are equal in his eyes'.[39] Jesus made this plain in the parable of the labourers in the vineyard, who were hired at different times of the day. They all received equal pay at the end of the day.[40] The reward here probably refers to the gift of eternal life, which is the same whether we have served him all our lives or come to faith shortly before death, as the thief who was crucified along with Jesus.[41] Whatever other rewards Christ will dispense, we can be confident that the Judge of all the earth will do what is right.[42]

Nature of the rewards

The rewards are spoken of using the metaphor of crowns. The 'crowns' to be dispensed at the *bëma* judgement are identified in Scripture as:

- 'A crown that will last for ever' for those who have kept their sinful nature in check.[43]
- 'A crown of righteousness' for those who long for Christ's coming again.[44]
- 'A crown of life' for those who have endured trial and testing, even unto death.[45]
- 'A crown of rejoicing' for those who have helped people into the kingdom.[46]
- 'A crown of glory' for those who have served God's people faithfully.[47]

While these are intangible 'crowns', they are real rewards and incentives to encourage us in our service for God.

There are other ways in which these rewards are expressed. It is not so much the success of our achievement that God is interested in, but our *faithfulness*.[48] In the parable of the talents, the more gifted servant who was entrusted with five talents and had gained five more received the same reward as the servant with only two talents and who gained two more. The reward that both these faithful servants received was the master's praise, a share in his happiness and the promise of further responsibilities: 'Well done, good and faithful servant! You have been faithful with a few things; I will put you in charge of many things. Come and share your master's happiness!'[49]

George Eliot wrote, 'The reward of one duty is the power to fulfil another.'[50] Part of our future reward as servants of God is to be given opportunity to continue to serve him for all eternity. In the revelation given to John of the future life in heaven we read, '*His servants will serve him*. They will see his face, and his name will be on their foreheads.'[51] So we finish this chapter on rewards of service where we began. Abraham's reward for obeying the call was God himself, and our reward for service is further service in the presence of God himself.

SUMMARY

We do not serve for a reward, but God loves to reward his servants. God himself is our chief reward, but a life of service will be richly rewarded in so many ways, both here on earth and in eternity to come.

REFLECTIONS AND EXERCISES

1. REWARDS   What does it mean to you that God has promised to be 'your very great reward' for following him? To what extent are you growing in your relationship with Christ, and how are you enjoying God as your reward?
• Share this together in your small group.

2. Take some time to reflect on the specific rewards for service for God that are mentioned in this chapter: health, pleasure and satisfaction.
• Write about this in your journal, and/or share your experiences in your small group.

3. DEVELOPMENT   Think of specific ways in which you have grown in maturity, emotionally or spiritually, as a result of developing prosocial behaviour. Reflect on factors in your background or that have influenced you positively or negatively towards other-centredness. Have you found becoming other-centred difficult?
• What are you doing specifically in your relationships to reach out to others prosocially? Discuss this in your small group. How can you help each other to become more other-centred?

4. YOUR CHURCH   If you are part of a church fellowship, how are you contributing towards building up 'body life' by serving one another? Can you think of ways that you could develop this more in your church community?

5. FRUIT FROM SERVICE   As you look back on your life, what fruit can you see from your service for God? How have you assessed this, and how have you expressed your joy?
• It would be good to talk this through in a group context, in

133

order to obtain a more objective review and to encourage one another towards future service.

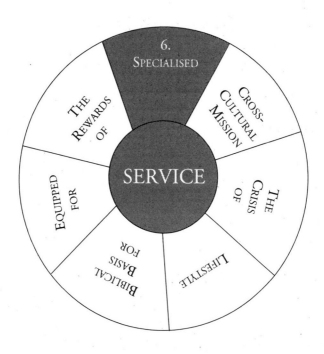

SERVICE

6. SPECIALISED

CROSS-CULTURAL MISSION

THE CRISIS OF

LIFESTYLE

BIBLICAL BASIS FOR

EQUIPPED FOR

THE REWARDS OF

Six

Specialised Service

*Meaning to life is not in competing and consuming,
but in contributing.*

Stephen Covey[1]

The true servant is someone who contributes positively to the lives of others. Many people do this daily, often unconsciously, through their normal work or profession. All jobs can be used either selfishly or for the benefit of others; they can be oriented towards how much I can gain or how much I can give. However, it is possible to earn a living in a profession, yet at the same time devote our lives and work to the benefit of others. We define these careers as the 'serving professions', and many people today are drawn towards them as ways of expressing their desire to serve others.

Of course, those not involved in one of these people-oriented occupations may have an equally strong servant attitude to life and be actively serving in many ways. We know some business people who spend their lives making money, yet use a significant proportion of their resources and energy to help others in need. We know others who see their job primarily as a way of providing the income to be able to serve God in their free time, or else to support other people to do so full time. Conversely, it is possible to be involved in one of the 'serving professions' but to be purely consumed by self-interest.

What a rare pleasure it is to be 'served' by a shop assistant, or waitress in a restaurant, who is genuinely interested in your needs and really sets out to meet them. There can be a big difference in the way a member of a service industry, such as a plumber, electrician or motor mechanic responds to your needs. Some merely do the job to earn a living, while others are genuinely concerned about the satisfaction of the customer.

THE SERVING PROFESSIONS

A large number of people in our society belong to the serving professions, meeting the needs of others. For many of them, it was this aspect of the work which appealed to them and drew them into this particular occupation. Certainly, they receive a salary for their work, and some may be more interested in the money or prestige that goes along with the job than in the individuals they work with. However, most of the people we know in the serving professions are there because they care about people. As one put it, 'I'm not there just to make a living but to make a difference.'

Some of the occupations we are defining as 'serving professions' can be well paid, but the majority of 'people-helping' jobs are not as highly remunerated as those which are primarily oriented towards making money. Maybe this says something about the value system of our society. In our world, profits often matter more than people.

We will refer briefly to some of the professions that are clearly involved with people in a serving capacity, but there will be others we have overlooked, either unintentionally or because of lack of space. In order to anchor our comments in reality, we have interviewed people who work in these professions to obtain their understanding of the service dimension of their job. We have combined their various comments in the different sections, and acknowledge the names of these resource people in the references.[2]

Nursing

The Christian Church has been involved in the care of sick people since early times. Fabiola, a Christian noblewoman of the fourth century, founded the first public hospital in Europe. However, it was not until the nineteenth century that Florence Nightingale established nursing in public hospitals as a dignified profession. She was a deeply committed Christian who wanted to serve in the church but was not given an opportunity, so decided to serve God in a secular setting.[3] She is recognised as a great figure in the history of nursing, and she established the first formal training courses.

Nursing care and midwifery was not only provided in hospitals but also in the community: in homes, industry, prisons and military establishments. Nursing used to be regarded as 'the handmaid of medicine', but over the past fifty years it has become recognised as a profession in its own right, with training ranging from basic courses to post-graduate degrees. Nursing always exists to alleviate suffering and bring comfort and healing to those who are physically and mentally ill.

I (Agnes) chose a nursing career as a way to express my faith through caring and service. My years of training were demanding but excellent preparation for the work ahead. I've always found so much satisfaction in giving myself through my nursing skills to sick people. When John and I planned to marry, we realised that combining our professions was a natural way to serve God together. This became a reality in our work for God in Papua New Guinea over a period of twenty-one years.

The following are comments from nurses we interviewed, who work in several branches of nursing: 'I see my life in nursing as worshipping the Lord through service. Nursing involves caring for the whole person. I believe healthy relationships with patients and the medical team are vital, especially in community nursing.' 'Nurses are often disadvantaged. I have loved every nursing job I've done, yet there is no romance in trying to be a Florence Nightingale – with irregular work hours, heavy responsibilities, low pay, facing singleness (especially for missionary nurses). However, there are many rewards: seeing intensely sick people recover, wounds heal, lives enriched, and sickness prevented through health education.'

'I found nursing older people stimulating, giving them the best send-off possible.' Another nurse struggled with 'wanting to allow people to die with dignity rather than keeping them alive with high tech equipment'. 'How are the patients I serve ever going to know what the gospel looks like if they don't see the love of Jesus in my actions.' 'Nursing is a demanding but satisfying profession.'

Medicine

The healing profession in all its many branches draws people who have a deep desire to alleviate suffering and combat disease or disability. Because people are human, these nobler desires can sometimes be contaminated by baser motives such as greed and seeking power or prestige. I'm aware that I (John) was attracted to the medical profession for quite the wrong reasons. I think my initial motives were because of the perceived social status attached to being a 'doctor', and because I needed to be needed in order to feel significant. However, as I grew in maturity and my commitment to Christ, these initial motivations were replaced by a deep desire to serve God and to serve people through medicine. This growth of awareness of the opportunities and privilege of serving others in this profession has also been the experience of other doctors we interviewed.

There is an infinite variety of branches of the medical profession, such as: family practice, specialties in medicine, surgery, obstetrics, public health, research, occupational health, tropical medicine, pathology, aviation medicine, to name a few. Some doctors are drawn to teaching and training others – in the role of a doctor/teacher: 'To train others so that they will become better than yourself.' This is appropriate, as the word 'doctor' means teacher, being derived from the Latin *docere*, to teach. Medical education is part of the job description of a doctor, whether one-to-one with a patient, in the community or training medical students to be good doctors and to treat people with respect, compassion and care. The following comments are from doctors we have interviewed:

'As a general practitioner, I enjoy being involved with others, and having a positive input in their lives. This takes me out of myself, and makes me appreciate the health and many blessings I have in my own life.' 'I appreciate the medical challenge and derive a buzz out of solving problems and seeing healing take place as a result, or at least the patient's quality of life improved.' 'My aims as a family practitioner, in a community at the lower end of the economic range, are to provide both good medicine and good care for people. I like to give as much time to individual patients as possible and to treat the whole person.'

Another GP said, 'I see the best way to serve my patients is by paying attention to mind, body and soul, because these cannot be separated. I tell them, "If you want me to be concerned only about your body, I may not be the right doctor for you." I do not see serving patients in terms of just providing comfort for them. Sometimes addressing the wider picture can be uncomfortable, but it leads to wholeness and healing.'

'I chose medicine because I wanted to serve God in a

141

practical way, with the goal of serving on the mission field.' 'The prime thing for me is the joy of serving a patient and bringing care and the qualities of Christ's love to a needy world.' 'My greatest reward was an awareness I was serving God in the place where he wanted me, and this enabled me to stay strong when the going was tough. I loved the challenge of medical problems in a Third World country, and seeing people recover in response to surgery. I developed many rewarding relationships with patients, as well as with the students and doctors I was training.'

Counselling/Psychotherapy

Over the second half of the twentieth century there were rapid advances in the fields of counselling and psychotherapy. Counselling has been defined as 'the art and science of helping people'. The emerging emphasis on the impact of emotional, social and spiritual factors on health and wellbeing is encouraging. There is also an increased willingness to address these issues, and to deal with 'baggage' from the past as well as struggles in the present. Seeking counselling help is a sign of strength, not weakness, indicating a desire to grow and mature as a person.

After twenty years in the medical and nursing professions, we re-trained in counselling in order to be able to minister to 'the whole person' more effectively.

We found it limiting and not fully satisfying to focus exclusively on the physical aspects of 'dis-ease', and gradually moved from clinical medicine to what we like to call *'people medicine'*. All disease is psycho-somatic. This means that psychological and somatic (physical) factors are part of the causation, development and healing of every illness.

Counselling is a process of helping people make personal changes in their lives by coming alongside them, listening, reflecting and occasionally challenging or providing information. Effective counsellors work *with* their clients but do not do the work for them. They are catalysts for change. Despite the popular view of counselling, the counsellor's task is not to give advice or solve problems, but to *empower* people to take responsibility for their lives. Counselling helps people gain insight into themselves and their difficulties, assisting them to grow to wholeness so that they can live more effectively in the future. Jesus came to make people whole and so he addressed the physical, social, emotional and spiritual needs of people.

Counselling is clearly a service profession, committed to the welfare of others. It can be hard work; at times rewarding and at other times discouraging. The counsellor sometimes feels like a garbage bin for others' unwanted rubbish. Counsellors can experience a sense of loneliness as they share, in confidence, other people's secrets and burdens. The counselling process is an experience of true intimacy between two people, but at the end, providing the counsellors have done their work well, clients move away to get on with their lives. This is as it should be, but counsellors are often left dealing with the loss of a meaningful relationship. True counselling has a cost attached, but this is counterbalanced by the satisfaction of being part of a healing process.

We asked a number of counsellors, 'What helps you continue in this demanding form of service?' They spoke of some of the 'rewards' of counselling: 'Seeing people putting their lives together, and then meeting them several years later and hearing about how the life changes they made have worked out.' 'I find it rewarding, especially as an older person, to work with people at the cutting edge of life, where stresses and changes are happening.' 'Seeing marriages come together and start to function well again is rewarding for me. Whenever appropriate, I also love to share the Lord – the ultimate Healer

– with others.' 'I am not the healer, just the one who brings others in touch with the Healer. This is the greatest reward.'

Social Work

Social workers provide assistance and advice to poor or disadvantaged members of society, and to people in crisis or following some tragedy. They also aim to influence attitudes in society so as to bring about positive changes in social and political structures. Their work involves helping people in a variety of situations, such as inadequate housing, poverty, rehabilitation from physical or mental illness, domestic problems, substance abuse and aging. Some social work agencies are run by the state and others by churches or charitable organisations. Social workers operate best as part of a team, including such professionals as the police, health care workers, counsellors, lawyers and others, utilising a network of resources. However, working constantly with people who often feel hopeless and stuck with insurmountable problems can be discouraging.

Most people involved in social work enjoy people and have a desire to serve others. One social worker said, 'A strong sense of call enabled me to cope when the task became difficult, giving me peace and a resolve to continue.' Others said that 'observing change and improved life outcomes for people' keeps them going. 'Seeing families come together is my greatest joy.' Hope is another important factor, essential for both for social workers and the people they work with. 'You have to be an optimist to be a social worker!'

Several we spoke to found the social-work system itself often limits their ability to achieve change, and they had to find ways of working 'outside the box', helping people to see other options and make choices. One neglected and often missing resource is the family, especially in western cultures. 'My major strategy is to focus on relationships and go out to meet the person or family where they are, rather than expecting them to be helped within our system. This works well with Maoris and Pacific Islanders.' 'I see social workers as the scaffolding, helping those involved in repairing a building. When the work is done we can pull away.'

Teaching

People become teachers for a variety of reasons. Many are attracted by the opportunity to have a positive input into young lives. For others, this aspect becomes more important as time goes by. A significant study was done by a sociologist in Florida in 1975, in which teachers were asked what attracted them to teaching. Themes that dominated their responses were: serving others, working with students and enjoyment of the job itself.[4] The service element of investing time and energy into the lives of pupils is possibly more important to teachers at the primary and secondary stage. This is because of a tendency at the tertiary level for some teachers to become more interested in the subject than in the student; in academic research rather than teaching.

Education *empowers* people, and assists the development of maturity. True learning is accompanied by growth in wisdom and character as well as knowledge. Teachers provide a powerful model for young people. One Principal defined his objective as: 'Aiming at producing better people, not just better marks.' Part of the attraction for some of the teachers we interviewed was finding creative and fun ways to teach: 'My goal is to help children enjoy learning, because when learning is fun it's likely to be more successful.' 'I have a deep and abiding fascination with how people grow, learn and change. Its exciting to know that the Holy Spirit is 'the Teacher', and when we work in partnership with him, people learn, grow and change more than we could ever expect.' 'I find it important to adjust my teaching methods to meet the needs of individual pupils, teaching them skills so they can continue learning on their own.'

Several teachers emphasised the importance of building good relationships with students, parents and staff. 'I find it rewarding to have students as friends in and out of school.' 'I think it's important to be who I am, up front as a real person with real values and make genuine relationships with my students. I'm aware there is a cost in being available to help students, both in and out of the classroom, and I'm learning to set appropriate boundaries.' The Principal of a large secondary school said, 'I believe in the servant–leadership model. My task is to promote excellence and high moral principles in the school, and to enable teachers at the chalk-face to do the best job they can.'

Law

The rule of law implies an ordered set of principles governing the actions of people, and that they are applied fairly and without favouritism. People or organisations who fail to conform to those principles can expect some kind of penalty. However, everyone accused of breaking the law, or who has been unjustly treated, has the right to adequate representation. The issue of human rights is an important stream of the law, to ensure all people are treated fairly and decently. At the end of the day, the legal process is all about people and their relationships with one another or the state. In this sense lawyers are part of a service profession and are there to serve the interest of their clients, although as in other professions, other motives may over-ride the service component.

The Greek *paraklētos* means intercessor, advocate, helper, mediator or one who appears on another's behalf. The word was occasionally used in literature to refer to an advocate or lawyer.[5] It is interesting that *paraklētos* is used to describe Jesus and the Holy Spirit.[6] The Holy Spirit comes alongside to take our part against the 'accuser' and before the 'Judge'.[7] This concept certainly describes the way a lawyer can exercise the servicing and caring aspect of his or her work. The following are some comments from lawyers we interviewed about their perceptions of the service aspect of their profession:

'What drew me towards being a lawyer was the opportunity to represent the interests of disadvantaged people in the community. I spent a number of years as a duty solicitor in criminal courts and as a legal aid lawyer. I enjoyed helping individuals, but now as a consultant, writer and teacher in the law school, I am still serving the community by trying to improve the system and ensure we have fair laws and policies.' 'My client is a government agency and I help it develop a framework of laws. My major motivation is to ensure the rights of all people, so that both the economically weak and the strong have the same protection.'

'I practise in the area of corporate and commercial law. In this business and financial field, I frequently remind myself that I am the kingdom of God in this situation.' 'As a litigation lawyer, I see myself as serving others, aiming to honour God in this situation. I find it rewarding to help resolve disputes with minimal acrimony.' 'I chose family law because I wanted to be involved with people, especially in times of difficulty. It is rewarding to help people unravel the confusion of the legal system, dispel fear, and assist them work through crises.'

'For me, the service component of my work is more related to how I practise my profession and how much I care for people, rather than what I do.'

Perhaps the ancient words from Proverbs sum up the work of lawyers: 'Speak up for people who cannot speak for themselves. Protect the rights of all who are helpless. Speak for them and be a righteous judge. Protect the rights of the poor and needy.'[8]

Serving Through Business

Businesses are set up with various objectives, the most common being to make as much money as possible. Clearly, a firm has to be profitable to survive, but when money becomes the 'driver', profits can take precedence over people. Some businessmen. however, see their major goal to be service to the community.

One classic example of this was *Robert Laidlaw*, who established an enterprise which eventually became The Farmers' Trading Company, based in Auckland.[9]

His aims were to provide a service to the farmers of New Zealand and become the largest mail order business in the country. Farmers all over the country could buy almost any commodity through them at a fair and competitive price, every item with a money-back guarantee.

Laidlaw regarded good service as the foundation on which a successful business is built. He wrote: 'Money doesn't make itself, it has to be made, and the necessary ingredients for making money may be all summed up in one word – service. Service is the cause, money the effect. He profits most who serves best.'[10] His stated aim for his company was: 'To serve the farmers in the best possible manner, with the best possible merchandise . . . and to absolutely satisfy every customer with every purchase.'[11]

Robert Laidlaw was a deeply committed Christian, who led many hundreds of people to faith in Christ. He gave unsparingly of his time and energy in the Lord's service, but gave also of his money. At the start of his business life, at eighteen, he decided to give 10 per cent of all he earned to the Lord. As his business prospered, he increased the proportion until by the time he was sixty he was giving 90 per cent of his income to the Lord's work.[12]

Dick Hubbard established a successful business in Auckland in 1988, Hubbard Foods Ltd, which produces mainly breakfast cereals and employs 120 people. He believes that a business must respond to all stakeholders: customers, staff, suppliers and the community as well as to the shareholders. He considers the success of their business is due to progressive management, acknowledging people and Christian values. The traditional model of business (as espoused by Adam Smith in his book *The Wealth of Nations,* 1776) is that business is driven by self-interest, greed and competition. Hubbard asserts that this concept is too narrow. 'Business is for the community and service must be part of the business world.' His firm is actively involved in helping schools and other agencies in the area.

In this connection he has set up an organisation known as Businesses for Social Responsibility, which currently has 170 member companies. Their goal is to encourage firms not only to help the community financially but also provide moral leadership and promote healthy attitudes. 'Businesses should focus on the *quality* of profit as well as the quantity, by providing a good human environment for people in their jobs rather than pushing the company's performance to the limit.' These views are gaining momentum worldwide, as British business columnist Charles Handy writes: 'We best satisfy ourselves when we look beyond ourselves.'

Dick Hubbard believes it is important to incorporate the basic family values of respect, caring and trust into a company. 'You can't expect people to be loving, caring parents at home if they spend all day in a cut-throat business looking after "Number One". The challenge is for businesses to operate on a moral basis that sets an example to the community. This is the essence of service.'

Writing

Writing books or articles may not seem at first glance to be a serving profession, as most writers ply their trade in solitude and do their best work when they are not relating to people. It can be lonely work. However, an author writes with people in mind, with the goals of entertaining, informing or challenging. Most writers have the interests of readers at heart, with a desire to enhance their lives in some way.

Through the pages of a book, it is possible to experience profound intimacy with another human being. We personally regard as 'friends' many authors we've never met, thinking some of their thoughts after them. Our goal as writers is to communicate ideas and truths that have changed our lives and which we want to share with others so that they too may be blessed. From letters and feed-back we have received, we know this happens. There are wonderful opportunities for Christians to serve with their pen (or word processor). Many people are discovering that they have this gift and are learning how to develop writing skills. Here are some comments from other writers:

Joyce Huggett, a well-known British author, expressed to us her motives for writing:

I write to inform, to inspire, to identify with the reader. I write, too, to pass on what I sense God is saying about a particular subject at a particular time. I write to promote growth, to impart wisdom and to serve my readers by implying, 'You can do it.' I write to underline the most healing message in the world: we are uniquely and unconditionally loved by God.

Julie Belding, an editor, writes:

When used in the service of God, writing is a powerful tool to persuade and encourage. Books, articles and letters have changed lives for good, but like all service, good writing is hard work, requiring practice and discipline. I believe the most important principle is this: you cannot write too clearly or too simply. If writing is your passion, ask God to show you how to serve him with this gift. Then, whether you are a letter writer, a novelist or an expert in some field, go out to bless your fellow human beings as God gives you opportunities.

Literature Promotion

There is not much point in writing books if they are not published, promoted and read. Some people are passionate about the value of literature and committed to the task of seeing good books produced and distributed widely. They find real meaning in a job that feeds minds with 'good food', and some booksellers go to great lengths to find the right book for a customer. However, the service aspect of this work is sometimes overshadowed by the struggle to survive financially in today's market. This can apply to author, publisher and bookseller alike.

Other factors at work are the trends for certain types of books, which fluctuate from time to time in the reading public. Some trends can be anticipated by the publisher but others are unpredictable. The Christian publisher must balance the desire to follow such fads with the call to publish material that will nourish people's minds and hearts. In order to survive, bookshops also tend to be customer driven, and are obliged to sell books from a wide range of publishers. It is important for Christian bookshops to stock a broad spectrum of books.

The *Christian bookshop* has an important service to offer the church and also provides a window of opportunity to the world. Unfortunately, churches do not always recognise this as a significant ministry, except perhaps in an overseas mission context. In fact, some churches see their bookshop as a 'cash cow' to finance other ministries, rather than an important main-street outreach into their community. Reliable surveys have shown that only about 20 per cent of Christians themselves actually make use of Christian bookshops

The degree of importance placed on promoting and reading good books is one reflection of the spiritual health of a church. Ways in which a church could encourage its fellowship to read would be through having a lending library, running a book stall, occasional short book reviews during services and giving appropriate books to people. The ministry of buying books to pass on to others is effective, as the saying goes: 'Give a gift that keeps on giving.'

Other Service Professions

All professions and trades have a significant service potential. For example, many people enter the arena of local or central government politics with a view to serving the community and promoting justice and progress. Others work in the relative obscurity of research and technology development for the benefit of humankind. The entertainment, sporting and travel industries are ultimately for the benefit of others, despite the fact that motivations for entering these professions could be more for fame or profit. Coaching young people in sport on a voluntary basis or running Scout or Brownie groups are examples of sacrificial service. It all depends on our value system. If my orientation is other-centred, there is no work, profession or interest in which I would be unable to serve.

HUMANITARIAN SERVICE

The Royal London Hospital where I (John) trained had the motto: *Nihil humani alienum puto*, which loosely translated from the Latin means, 'Because I am human, all things human interest me'. I have always found that a challenging maxim to try and live by – not only to have an interest in people but to be concerned about their needs. God is certainly like that.

God's Concern for the Poor

There are over 150 references throughout the Old and New Testaments about God's concern for the poor and needy, strangers and marginalised people in society and, at the same time, our responsibility to them is pointed out. God seems to place great importance on the degree of concern and care that we have for them too. For example:

> Defend the cause of the weak and fatherless; maintain the rights of the poor and the oppressed.[13]
> There will always be poor people in the land. Therefore I command you to be open-handed towards your brothers and towards the poor and needy.[14]
> He who is kind to the poor lends to the LORD, and he will reward him for what he has done.[15]

Jesus identified with the poor when he chose to enter this world in a humble, insignificant home. He was born in a cave, or place set aside for sheltering animals, and was brought up in a poor village. Thirty years later, when he announced his manifesto, the poor were right at the top of his list:

> 'The Spirit of the Lord is on me, because he has anointed me to preach good news to the poor. He has sent me to proclaim freedom for the prisoners and recovery of sight for the blind, to release the oppressed, to proclaim the year of the Lord's favour.'[16]

Later, when John the Baptist questioned whether Jesus really was the promised Messiah, as part of the evidence Jesus assured John that he was preaching to the poor, as well as performing miracles.[17]

Today, a quarter of the world's people still live in poverty and most of them go to bed hungry every night. Children are the main victims of poverty; 160 million children worldwide are moderately to severely malnourished. The rich are still getting richer and the poor becoming poorer; 1.3 billion people earn less than two dollars a day.[18] Most Christians in the West live in comparative affluence. God's concern for the poor has not changed, but perhaps ours has. Some Christians are deeply concerned about poverty and hunger and do something about it, but many others of us have learned to rationalise our affluence with only a casual thought for those in need. A challenging book which tackles this issue is *Rich Christians in an Age of Hunger* by Ronald Sider.[19]

During the twentieth century, a growing number of voluntary agencies were set up in the western world to do something about the needs of those less fortunate.

Private Voluntary Organisations (PVOs)

These are sometimes known as *Nongovernment Organisations* (NGOs), or third party organisations, because they exist to serve the needs of people who are not themselves members of the organisations. These agencies are all an expression of voluntary action, and are concerned with human welfare in such fields as health, the environment and economics. Some of them are the result of the Church's desire to serve needy people, but others have been set up by secular agencies. However, most of them originated in 'Christian countries', and reflect the influence of biblical values still existing in societies which are now mainly post-Christian. They all provide an opportunity to serve others.

The first recorded example of organised voluntary relief of suffering was the fund Paul set up for the relief of poor

Christians in Jerusalem by the churches in Asia.[20] There have been isolated examples of this sort of thing over the centuries. In 1642 Irish Protestant Christians sent food to North America to help settlers and victims of war. In the eighteenth and nineteenth centuries British Christian charities sent support to missionaries in America and schools for Indians and blacks. During World War I, a number of charities were set up in the US to send food to Europe. The oldest British international assistance charity, Save the Children Fund, was founded in 1919.[21]

Over the last few years there has been a rapid proliferation of PVOs in many countries. This is because 'we live in a world of dehumanising poverty, collapsing ecological systems and deeply stressed social structures'.[22] These NGOs can be divided into three 'generations', each with different strategies.[23]

a) *First generation* voluntary development action is responding to immediate needs, such as caring for starving children or people devastated by earthquakes and floods. The beneficiaries are passive recipients.

b) *Second generation* strategies focus on communities, helping them become self-reliant. Many NGOs start off providing immediate aid and then move on to second generation strategies, assisting communities to meet their own needs. The focus is on education and technical assistance rather than handouts; partnership not paternalism.

c) *Third generation* strategies look beyond individual communities, seeking changes and improvement in the welfare of people at the local, national and international level. This transformation is harder, takes longer and may be resisted by governments which prefer handouts to change.

Service Clubs

The idea of civilian service clubs originated with Paul Harris, a young Chicago attorney, when he founded Rotary International in 1905. The purpose was to foster 'the ideal of service' as a basis of enterprise, and their motto is: 'Service Above Self'. Membership of any particular local Rotary club is restricted to a single representative from each profession, business and institution in the community. There are now over 28,000 local Rotary clubs in 154 countries. Most of them meet weekly.

Other clubs of somewhat similar design followed, such as the Kiwanis in 1915 and Lions in 1917, and many other associations of service clubs for both men and women. Service clubs around the world carry out several hundred thousand projects, ranging from educational scholarships to camps for underprivileged children; responding to hunger, poverty and a great variety of community needs. Such clubs provide a forum for people to express their desire to serve others, particularly the less fortunate in the community. Many Christians belong to service clubs, as do people who have no religious beliefs. Working together for a common goal provides a bond and fellowship, as well as opportunities for sharing one's faith.

Special Needs Support Groups

Within most communities, especially in large cities, there are numerous support organisations and groups run mostly by volunteers. We counted 270 of them listed in one Auckland region directory, ranging from Alcoholics Anonymous to Women's Refuges.[24] Many groups support people suffering from specific illnesses or disabilities (or their friends or relatives who care for them) such as: Alzheimer's disease, AIDS, blindness, brain injury victims, deafness, Down's syndrome, epilepsy, infertility, multiple sclerosis, schizophrenia and many more.

Others are concerned with addiction problems, such as alcohol, drugs, gambling or overeating. Various telephone counselling agencies have been developed over the past forty years, such as Life Line and Samaritans. We ourselves worked as Life Line counsellors and supervisors for a number of years. Many telephone counselling services or help-lines have been established to meet different needs in the community.

Traditionally, a variety of groups have been available to support women. More recently there has been a growing interest in the problems men face, with the development of men's support groups and counselling agencies, anger management training, Men Against Violence and groups for men with sexual addiction or sexual abuse problems. Men are often reluctant to admit they have a problem and unwilling to seek help, but these attitudes are changing. Many counselling agencies are now available in the community to provide help for individuals or families.

This list of special-need agencies represents a growing interest in the community to care for and serve those who are disadvantaged.

SERVING WITHIN THE CHURCH

Office Bearers in the Church

In Chapters One and Three we identified commitment to service as a hallmark of the Christian who seeks to follow Jesus, the Servant King. This is especially true of the leaders in the church, who are called to servant leadership. The terms used in many churches for their designated leaders are minister and deacon, both of them meaning servant. Other churches define their leaders as priests. While it is true that all true believers are called to be priests,[25] the priest in leadership of a congregation is to be there for others, as a 'shepherd of the flock'. If the leaders of the church model service in their ministry, others will follow.

Full-time church leaders are usually paid, though mostly at

a considerably lower rate than what might be earned in secular work. In many smaller churches, those in leadership may also be in secular employment. However, as the fellowship grows in numbers, it is more efficient to have full-time pastors or ministers and administration staff, but this does not mean that the other members of the congregation need now serve less. In fact, part of the function of good church leadership is to recognise and encourage the gifts within the congregation and to co-ordinate the service of each member of the fellowship.

Other Church-Related Ministries

There are many and varied ways in which all members of a congregation can serve within the church. In Chapter Four we looked at the spiritual gifts, and noted that each believer is provided with at least one of them. Paul tells us these gifts have been given 'to prepare God's people for works of service, so that the body of Christ may be built up'.[26] Peter wrote that 'each one should use whatever gift he has to serve others'.[27] So, clearly, there is provision for each one of us to serve within our local church fellowship. The more members of a church are involved in service, the more vital that church will be and the greater impact it will have in its community.

Many fellowships have some members who are in full-time Christian ministry outside the church structure. They attend church primarily to be 'watered and fed' and have their spiritual batteries recharged, so that they can perform their service for the Lord more effectively. However, it is still healthy for them, and for the church, if they are also involved in some aspect of service within the fellowship. This may be in only a small way, such as being part of a specialist advisory committee, involved in prayer ministry, contributing to the services occasionally, singing in the choir, preaching, leading a home group, offering hospitality or pastoral care. 'Now you are the body of Christ,'

Paul wrote, 'and *each one* of you is a part of it.'[28] However, much Christian service is done today outside the structure of the church.

PARA-CHURCH ORGANISATIONS

The term 'para-church' is defined as 'an organisational tradition of Christian associations that lie outside the church in terms of structure and accountability'.[29]

These agencies are usually staffed by Christians and are committed to specific aspects of extending Christ's kingdom, but are not primarily involved in the work of the church. There are many such organisations, serving people in different ways. Some of them are run by a denomination or a local church, such as a social-work agency, retirement home or counselling service. The people working in these organisations may or may not all belong to that particular church. Other para-church organisations are intentionally inter-denominational in terms of staffing and support.

There was a steady increase in these 'special purpose groups' during the second half of the twentieth century. The three main emphases of these agencies are:

a) *Mission,* such as a missionary society, The Bible Society, The Gideons.
b) *Education,* such as Bible Schools or Colleges, Christian schools.
c) *Humanitarian,* such as World Vision or TEAR Fund.

A number of organisations have been set up to work specifically with young people, such as the YMCA, Student Christian Movement, InterVarsity Fellowship, Scripture Union, Navigators, Campus Crusade for Christ and Christian holiday camps.

The term para-church literally means 'alongside the church'. Unfortunately, these groups sometimes appear to be in opposition to the church, and certainly compete for personnel and money, because they both draw on the same resources.[30] Sometimes the para-church organisation provides a fellowship which meets the spiritual needs better for Christians who do not feel comfortable in a formal church, or whose gifts are not being utilised within the church. Para-church ministries provide opportunity for many Christians to express their desire for service. Of many such organisations, we have selected three to describe.

Christian Care Centre

When we returned from missionary service in Papua New Guinea, we felt called to set up an agency that was committed to caring for the whole person: spiritually, physically, emotionally, mentally and socially. The goal was to mobilise Christians with a range of professional skills to work together reaching from the church into the community. The staff of the *CCC* came from a variety of churches, and at one stage we had a team of about twenty people, representing eight different denominations. The plan was to base our programme around a medical practice and offer a range of other services, such as professional counselling, physiotherapy, occupational therapy, drug rehabilitation, social work, legal aid and budgeting advice.

We rented an old house in a densely populated suburb, bought for the purpose by a Christian trust. Initially all our staff were part-time and gave their services voluntarily, earning their living professionally elsewhere. Eventually, we were able to generate enough income from medical and counselling fees to support a few full-time personnel. At the beginning, we offered all the services mentioned above, but the social work aspects were being catered for quite well by the local council, so we decided not to compete in these areas.

Our main work centred around a medical and counselling

practice, with two or three doctors, nurses and up to six trained psychotherapists. We worked closely together as a 'healing team', offering comprehensive whole-person care. Another aspect we developed was a range of seminars and training courses, such as: marriage enrichment, stress management, communication, conflict resolution, coping with depression, building self-esteem and basic people-helping skills. Several thousand people attended these courses over the years, and this proved to be an effective way of helping church congregations as well reaching out into the community.

The Centre ran for sixteen years, and was almost entirely self-supporting. However, it was a struggle to meet the costs of such an agency from our own resources, because most of our patients and clients were drawn from the lower end of the economic scale. We had a policy of never turning away anyone who could not pay the full fees.

When we started there was nothing available of this nature in New Zealand, but by the time we closed a number of other similar centres had started up around the country, reflecting variations of the CCC model, which was encouraging. The Christian Care Centre provided an opportunity for many of us to express our faith by serving others. One of our team expressed it well in a poem:

> There is heart-ache throbbing in the city,
> There is heart-break stalking the land.
> There's a call for hearts of human pity
> To reach out a healing hand.
> I hear a mother who's weeping
> For a child that she must mourn,
> Buried hopes are creeping
> Into a heart that's torn.

I see a husband's deep anguish
For a partner who has left,
Leaving him to languish,
Achingly bereft.

I know a family hurting
Because of love unexpressed,
The hurting projected as hating,
Assuaged by forgiveness expressed.

I feel a community crumbling,
As violence and lies multiply,
People are struggling and stumbling;
For meaning and hope they cry.

There is heart-ache throbbing in the city,
There is heart-break stalking the land.
There's a call for hearts of human pity
To reach out – a healing band!

Gordon Hambly

World Vision

This agency was started in 1950 by Dr Bob Pierce, initially to provide emergency care for war orphans in Korea. It is now an international Christian aid and development organisation, working in over one hundred countries in the world with needy people, regardless of race, religion or creed. World Vision currently resources well over 5,000 projects, as diverse as providing communities with clean water, building and equipping schools, improving agriculture yields and leadership development.[31]

The emphasis of WV is on rehabilitation and development in communities. The main means of funding is through child sponsorship, linking children with individual donors to bring food, medical help, education and hope to many thousands of children and their families. World Vision believes in the concept of 'transformational development – empowering people to transform their world'. This encourages people to solve their problems themselves with whatever help they need. A recent example was a project funded by WV New Zealand in India, assisting people build a dam to provide water in an area where for lack of it the population had to migrate several months each year. By providing food in exchange for work, the local people completed the job of building the dam themselves in the dry season. When Colin Prentice (WVNZ Director) attended the opening ceremony, he saw a notice that had been erected with pride: 'We have done it ourselves with the help of World Vision.'

Emergency relief is an important aspect of WV ministry, and they respond promptly to disasters resulting from earthquakes, floods, war or famine. Addressing the needs of children worldwide, such as feeding programmes, caring for street kids and attempting to combat the sexual exploitation of children, is a major aspect of the work. A significant proportion of World Vision support is also raised by school children, through the annual '40-Hour Famine' appeal.

Colin started working with World Vision six years ago after a successful teaching career. He speaks of the sheer joy and happiness in being part of a serving ministry that works with the poor and marginalised, especially in giving children a fresh start in life. He is constantly amazed at the faith, dedication and sacrifice of World Vision field staff; both those from the sending countries and the national team members. There is room for many more to join them, expressing their faith through loving action!

The following comments are from Suzanne Wavre

(currently WV Director for South Africa) who has worked for World Vision for twenty-three years.

This has provided a fulfilling, exciting and varied career for me in many places. I started out in West and then Southern Africa, and was in Sahel during the dreadful droughts of the mid-eighties, when thousands of people starved to death in the desert. We drove ourselves to physical, emotional and spiritual limits trying to save lives, especially of children. While working in the international liaison office in Geneva, I helped with the Romanian orphan support programme. I established the WV development programme in Mongolia, after the fall of the Soviet Union in the nineties. For the last four years I have directed the WV programme in Vietnam.

My motivation to serve is rooted in a Christian heritage and the example of my missionary parents and grandparents. There is nothing romantic about serving others in far off, lonely, uncomfortable and often dangerous assignments. Working with people who have a totally different culture and world view, or battling frustrating bureaucracy is not easy. But I love the challenge of bringing hope and the possibility of a better future, physically and spiritually, to many who never dreamed of such things. When we reach outside ourselves with joy and enthusiasm to others, God creates new perspectives within us.

Prison Ministries[32]

Many Christians visit prisons to share with inmates friendship, love and the knowledge of life to be found in Jesus. One of the larger organisations involved in this work is Prison Fellowship International, founded in 1976 by Charles Colson after his own experience in prison.[33] Their motto is, 'A bruised reed he will not break, and a smouldering wick he will not snuff out.'[34] This organisation also works with the families of those in prison and with ex-prisoners, who need much support in their rehabilitation. The third aspect of the work of PFI is to bring about reconciliation and restoration of the criminal justice system.[35] They work in over eighty countries and have thousands of trained volunteers and many assistant chaplains who visit prisons.

Visiting prisons is not glamorous work. It requires time and patience, but it is rewarding. I (John) have visited some prisoners, but here are a few comments from people who have spent a lot of time in this service for the Lord. 'There is freedom behind bars: forgiveness and relief to be found in Christ. Over eighteen years we've seen murderers, rapists, Satanists and gang members saved by the One who came "to proclaim freedom to prisoners".'[36] 'Prisons have been described as "hell-holes", yet for some they become the gate to heaven.' 'One man, who had "HELL" tattooed in large letters on his forehead, told me of the forgiveness and love he had found in Christ while in prison.'

Prison visitation is demanding work, but can be so effective and rewarding. 'After returning from a visit I am reminded of the words of Jesus, "I was in prison and you came to visit me." '[37] 'It continues to be a wonderful encouragement to my faith to meet prisoners who have been radically changed in their attitudes, direction and values on coming to a personal faith in Jesus.'

A prison chaplain writes:

> Bent and bruised people can be restored to shalom, and visitation of prisoners by Christians is a significant help in this process. One of the greatest rewards of my work is to see men hungering to know the Lord and finding direction and purpose in their lives.

Prison ministries bring together dedicated people from different traditions of the Christian faith in a challenging but exciting service for God.

SUMMARY

In this chapter we looked at many ways in which service can be provided in our everyday lives and work. Christians do not have a monopoly on service or caring for the poor and needy, but they are at the forefront of this way of life, working both in specifically Christian and in secular organisations. Serving others in the name of Christ is the prime way in which our faith can be put into practice and made relevant to a needy world.

REFLECTIONS AND EXERCISES

1. SERVING AT WORK   In what ways have you been able to serve God and others through your profession or work? What opportunities are you finding in your everyday working life to be a servant to others and share your faith in practical ways? In what ways could you develop more of a servant lifestyle?
- It would be helpful to discuss these questions with your small group or friends.

2. THE POOR   To what degree do you share God's concern for the poor and needy?
- Make a study of what the Bible has to say on this topic, especially in the OT prophets and the epistles. The epistles of James and John, and the second half of Paul's letters deal with this issue.
- Check out your own community for opportunities to be part of a humanitarian organisation or service club that is appropriate for your gifts.

3. THE CHURCH   There are many opportunities for service in the church. Perhaps you are already involved in your church in some way, but if not this might be something you would like to consider. (See the section on discovering your spiritual gifts in Chapter Four.)

4. PARA-CHURCH   There is likely to be some para-church organisation that could really benefit from your skills. Why not explore the possibilities?

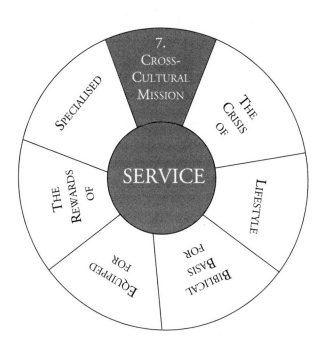

SERVICE

7. CROSS-CULTURAL MISSION

THE CRISIS OF

LIFESTYLE

BIBLICAL BASIS FOR

EQUIPPED FOR

THE REWARDS OF

SPECIALISED

Seven

Cross-Cultural Mission Service

*He is no fool who gives what he cannot keep
to gain what he cannot lose.*

Jim Elliott[1]

The story is told of the time Jesus returned to heaven and reported back on his mission to earth and all he had accomplished. There was silence for a while, then one of the senior angels asked,

'Lord, what plans do you have for the spread of the gospel throughout the earth?'

Jesus replied, 'I spent three years training a small band of men and women. One of them betrayed me, but the others love me and will be my witnesses. They will take the Good News to the world.'

The angel asked again, 'But what if they fail you. Do you have any contingency plans?'

'No, I have no other plan.'

Mission is at the heart of the purposes of God on earth. God chose Abraham and the Israelite nation in order to bless 'all peoples of the earth'.[2] They failed in this task, but what about us, the people of the new covenant? The last recorded words of our Saviour before returning to heaven were:

> 'But you will receive power when the Holy Spirit comes upon you; and you will be my witnesses in Jerusalem, and in all Judea, and Samaria, and to the ends of the earth.'[3]

After two millennia, this command has only partially been obeyed. There are an estimated 5 million Christian workers in their home countries compared with just over 0.4 million foreign missionaries. This is a ratio of 1:12, or approximately one missionary representing 4,800 Christians at home.[4] It is estimated that less than 1 per cent of church spending goes to frontline mission work.

It took persecution to drive out the early Christians from Jerusalem and scatter them throughout Judea, Samaria and to the ends of the earth.[5] As they travelled, they spread the Good News.[6] The Greek word used here can be variously translated: 'tell', 'proclaim' or 'converse with'. In fact, they mainly just 'gossiped the gospel' as they went. Similarly, as the above statistics indicate, most Christian service today takes place in our 'Jerusalems' or 'Judeas', i.e. primarily among people who are already Christians or have been heavily evangelised. The number of individuals who have not heard the gospel has increased over this past century from 813 million to 1,530 million.[7]

A BRIEF HISTORY OF CHRISTIAN MISSIONARY SERVICE[8]

The woman of Samaria could be regarded as the very first missionary, and many Samaritans responded to her testimony.[9] This paved the way for the missionary endeavours of Philip, Peter and John among the Samaritans later.[10] Paul and Barnabas formed the first planned missionary team. In about AD 45 they were sent out by the church in Antioch, under the inspiration of the Holy Spirit.[11] This was some twelve years after Jesus had returned to heaven. The book of Acts covers the way the gospel spread to the Middle East and Europe over the next twenty-four years, mainly describing the missionary work of Paul and his companions.

The other apostles, as well as many other 'missionaries', would no doubt have been specifically sent out, and thousands of believers scattered in all directions. According to tradition, Matthew went to Ethiopia, Andrew to Scythia (Russia), Bartholomew to Arabia, Peter to Spain, Mark to Africa, John and Philip to Europe and Thomas to India. Certainly the church of South India dates from a very early era, attributed to the missionary work of St Thomas.

Eusebius of Caesarea (260–340) wrote about the spread of the gospel by many Christians in the beginning of the second century: 'Their first action in obedience to the instructions of the Saviour was to sell their goods and distribute them to the poor. Then, leaving their homes, they set out to fulfil the work of an evangelist, making it their ambition to preach the word of faith to those who as yet had nothing of it.'[12] Women played a prominent part in the expansion of the Church during the first five centuries and many were martyred. The loving service and care shown by Christians probably had as big an impact on people as the message they preached.

Despite (or because of) the incredible persecution of the Christians unleashed by Nero and other Roman emperors, the Church spread rapidly, particularly among poorer people. 'By the end of the third century there was no part of the Roman Empire which had not been to some extent penetrated by the Gospel.'[13] Reliable estimates place the number of Christians at 10 per cent of the total population of the empire by the year 313. Factors that assisted the spread of the gospel were the relative stability of life in the Roman Empire, good roads, the almost universal use of the Greek language and the use of Jewish synagogues as starting points for evangelism.

Evangelisation into Europe

The whole situation changed dramatically at the beginning of the fourth century, when the Emperor Constantine (274–337) became open to the Christian faith and was baptised. The Church now became popular, but was in danger of being submerged under a flood of new believers, many of whom had only a superficial faith. However, it was during this period that the basic doctrines were formulated by outstanding leaders, and affirmed at the Council of Nicea (325) and other forums.

Christianity spread to many places beyond the Roman Empire. Early in the third century the gospel reached north-west to Armenia and to the Goths in Europe, inspired and led by the outstanding missionary work of Ulifas (311–382). By the fifth century, Christianity was well established in France, England and Ireland. The missionary zeal of monks from Ireland brought the faith to Scotland and Columba established a monastery in Iona, from which the gospel spread out into Scotland and England. The evangelistic emphasis of the Celtic Christians had a great impact throughout England and Europe in succeeding years. In 596 a significant missionary outreach was initiated when Pope Gregory the Great dispatched Augustine and his party of monks to Britain, making their base in Canterbury.

AD 500–1500

During what is known as the 'Dark Ages', Christianity spread from England into the countries of Europe. Perhaps the greatest missionary of this period was Boniface (680–754) who led a team of missionaries to the German lands. By the turn of the first millennium Russia had adopted Christianity as a result of an outreach by the Orthodox Church in Constantinople.

The rise of the Muslim tide from 622 on was a major disaster for Christendom, sharply curtailing Christian witness. One of the most remarkable Christian missionary stories of the Medieval period was the penetration into China by the Nestorians (a group of Christians based in Persia) who reached the heart of China by 635. Their influence grew over the next 200 years, until the monks were expelled by Emperor Wu Tsuang in 845.

The Christian Church not only had to contend with the Muslim threat from the South, but also the destruction and setback caused by the Vikings and Danes in the North. In the 790s they started pillaging England, Ireland and Europe, destroying churches, monasteries and Bibles. However, many captives taken by the Vikings as wives and serfs were Christians and, amazingly, within 200 years most of Scandinavia had become at least nominally Christian. The same could be said for most of Europe. The problem was that much Christianity was based upon the enforcement of it by rulers.

An unfortunate outcome of the upsurge of the Church in Europe was the Crusades (1096–1204) – an attempt to deliver the holy places from the hands of unbelievers. The Crusades were a shameful disaster, resulting in bitterness with Muslims that continues to this day. In the thirteenth century another great threat descended on 'Christian' Europe in the form of the Mongolian hordes from the East. However, the Church gained considerable influence with various Great Khans, and a number of their princesses and court officials became Christians.

There were many attempts during the Middle Ages to take the gospel to various parts of the world. The Franciscan and Dominican orders, which arose during the twelfth century, had a missionary vision. St Francis (1181–1226) began missions to Egypt, Syria and North Africa. Over the next hundred years

Franciscan missionaries reached to the ends of the then known earth. Ramón Lull (1235–1315) was a scholar and linguist, particularly interested in the Semitic languages; and until he was martyred he pioneered 'evangelism by reasoning' with the Muslims.

The Sixteenth Century

During this period, called 'the Age of Discovery', enormous changes took place in the world and in the Church. Portuguese and Spanish explorers sailed east and west. Christopher Columbus crossed the Atlantic to the Bahamas in 1492. As hitherto unknown worlds were explored and opened up to trade, the Church took advantage of this to spread the gospel. The Jesuit order, founded by Ignatius of Loyola in 1534, sent missionaries to many countries, in particular India, Japan and South America. The most famous was Francis Xavier who went to India in 1542, then on to Malacca and finally to Japan. There was a significant response in Japan, with an estimated 300,000 baptised believers. However, in the seventeenth century, ferocious persecution by the shogûns eliminated most of them.

Francis Xavier hoped to enter China, but never did. Three hundred years earlier Friar John had reached China under the protection of the Mongols. As a result of his preaching thousands were baptised. However, under the Ming dynasty all missionaries were expelled and Christians eliminated. Another Jesuit missionary, Matteo Ricci (1552–1610) went first to the Portuguese island of Macao, where he learned Chinese. Later he was invited by the emperor to Peking. He adopted the dress of a Confucian scholar and reached many intellectuals, some 2,000 professing to become Christians, but by 1724 all missionaries were again expelled from China. During the same period, Jesuit missionaries accompanied the Spanish and

Portuguese conquests of Central and South America. The military invaders of the New World treated the local people with great cruelty, and in turn the Indians often massacred missionaries.

On 31st October, 1517, Martin Luther posted his ninety-five theses on the door of the Wittenburg church. This launched the Reformation, which had tremendous impact on the Church. However, this was not followed immediately by an interest in missions by Protestant churches. In fact, Luther was so convinced of the imminent return of Christ that he was not interested in foreign missions.

The Seventeenth and Eighteenth Centuries

Roman Catholic missions continued, particularly in the New World. Protestant interest in missionary work among the Indians was sparked off by John Eliot (1604–1690), followed by David Brainerd (1718–1747). One of the greatest missionary statesmen of the eighteenth century was the German Count Zinzendorf (1700–1760) who founded the Moravian Brethren, which sent out hundreds of missionaries with a deep love for Christ and passion for evangelism.

The Nineteenth Century

This was truly 'the great century' of Christian advance.[14] The evangelical revivals that began in England with Whitfield and Wesley resulted in a new awareness of the need for worldwide evangelism. William Carey (who is often spoken of as 'the father of modern missions') arrived in India in 1793. A number of missionary societies were founded, such as the English Baptists in 1792, the London Missionary Society in 1795, the Church Missionary Society in 1799 and many others followed.

Secular trends also had an impact. 'The Age of Enlightenment and eighteenth-century rationalism had been largely replaced by a new Age of Romanticism.'[15] The Industrial Revolution in Europe brought new power, and with it an urge to conquer. This was the era of colonial expansion. While this made missionary enterprise easier, it also caused confusion by associating Christianity with imperialism and colonialism, both in the attitudes of the missionaries and the eyes of those they worked among.

Many of the men and women, whose names are etched forever in the missionary roll of honour, set out for foreign lands during this era. Here are brief sketches of a few, whose biographies make exciting and challenging reading.

1806. *Henry Martyn* went to India and Persia. In the six years before he died he translated the New Testament into Hindustani, Arabic and Persian.

1807. *Robert Morrison* was the first Protestant missionary to China, though he was only able to be there as an employee of the East India Company in Canton. He translated the Bible into Chinese.

1812. *Adoniram and Ann Judson* were America's first Protestant foreign missionaries. They went to India, then on to Burma. He translated the Bible into Burmese. As a family they suffered much and Adoniram was imprisoned for eighteen months in a filthy 'death-row' gaol.

1817. *John and Mary Williams* went to Tahiti and evangelised all the islands of that group, with the aid of ships and trained native evangelists. He was murdered and eaten in 1839 while visiting an island in the New Hebrides.

1829. *Anthony and Mary Groves* with their two boys left in a small yacht, sailing as far as St Petersburg, and then went overland to Bagdad. Mary died from the plague two years later. Anthony Norris Groves moved to India and established a number of churches there. He died in 1853.

1841. *David Livingstone* followed Robert Moffatt to Africa, and became the most well-known and honoured missionary and explorer of the century. His African friends found him dead, kneeling by his cot, one morning in 1873. They buried his heart under a mpundu tree, mummified his body in the sun and carried it to the coast. He was given a state funeral in Westminster Abbey, London.

1854. *Hudson Taylor* sailed for China at the age of twenty-one. He concentrated on itinerant evangelism and adopted Chinese dress and culture. Within fifty years, the mission he founded (CIM) had over 600 missionaries working in every province of China.

1866. *James ('Tamate') and Jane Chalmers* set sail for Rarotonga, and after ten years went to New Guinea. He had a wonderful way with the local people, but unfortunately on a trip to the Fly River region in 1901 he was killed and eaten.

1876. *Mary Slessor* went to Nigeria, and did an amazing pioneering work for nearly forty years. She lived mostly in a mud hut 'native-style', and, along with her other missionary duties, became a peacemaker and judge among the African people.

1893. *Amy Carmichael* went to Japan and then to Sri Lanka and India, where she established the Dohnavur Fellowship, and rescued hundreds of temple children from lives of prostitution. She had a big impact though her books.

In 1861 Royal Wilder, a missionary in India, asserted that 'the church of Christ is able to evangelise the whole world in one short generation'.[16] This became the slogan of the Student Volunteer Movement, which was founded in 1886. Perhaps the most famous student volunteer was the cricketer, C.T. Studd, who went to China as part of what became known as the 'The Cambridge Seven'. He later worked in Africa and founded the Worldwide Evangelisation Crusade (now WEC

International). The Student Volunteer Movement had a great appeal to students in North America, Britain and Europe. It has been estimated that over a period of fifty years, SVM was responsible for over 20,000 students going to the mission field.

The Twentieth Century

This past century has been a tumultuous time, with more changes, discoveries and development than in the whole previous history of humankind.[17] The technological revolution happens so fast today that its not possible to keep up with it. Human beings have discovered how to travel in space, but not how to live peacefully on earth. Over the past one hundred years there have been two world wars and we have seen the rise and demise of Communism. Even though it is more than half a century since World War II, there has not been a time since then without fighting and conflict in different parts of the world. Colonialism is now almost a thing of the past as more and more countries have achieved independence from foreign domination.

Through all of this, missionary endeavour has stayed alive and well, although missionary methods have had to adapt and become more flexible. One feature of the nineteenth and twentieth centuries has been the rise of 'faith missions'. In 1829, Anthony Norris Groves set the pattern for missionaries from Open Brethren Assemblies (now CMML, Christian Missions in Many Lands) to go to almost every part of the world in faith, trusting the Lord for their needs and with no guarantee of a regular salary. The Zenana Bible and Medical Mission (now Interserve) started in 1852, and the China Inland Mission (now OMF International) in 1865.

These were followed by many others, such as the Christian and Missionary Alliance in 1887, Sudan Interior Mission (now SIM International) in 1893, and New Tribes Mission in 1942. Scores of independent 'faith missions' were formed to reach different groups around the world. These missions have been associated mostly with conservative evangelical churches with a strong emphasis on evangelism and church planting.

Denominational missions, particularly the Anglican, Baptist, Catholic, Presbyterian, Methodist, Salvation Army, Open Brethren and Pentecostal churches have all been active in sending out missionaries. Interdenominational missions, of course, all draw on these churches for their recruits. A survey taken in the mid-1980s showed a range of interest in overseas mission by different denominations worldwide.

Anglican	11	Baptist	61	Brethren	88
Pentecostal	36	Methodist	6	Presbyterian	3
		Salvation Army	34		

Number of missionaries per 10,000 church members[18]

Conclusion:

Ralph Winter has summarised the pattern of conflict and expansion of the Christian Church in five blocks of approximately 400 years.[19]

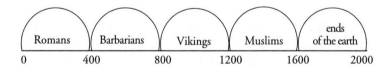

Not all of this history was honouring to God, but history illustrates the unstoppable advance of the kingdom. God continues to bless the spread of his word, despite our human frailty.

The purpose of this brief review of the history of Christian missions is to provide a challenge concerning the work that remains to be done. It is also encouraging to realise that we build today on 2,000 years of dedicated missionary endeavour. Missionary emphasis has changed from pioneer evangelism to partnership with indigenous churches by invitation. Missionaries are the *scaffolding*; the building is the kingdom of God.

National churches are not only managing their own affairs, but are sending out missionaries themselves to other lands. Receiving countries are now sending countries. For example, a fast growing area of mission at this time is in India, with Indians working cross-culturally. The need for the Church universal to find effective ways to be involved in mission is greater than ever as we enter the third millennium.

SPECIALISED MISSION MINISTRIES

One feature of twentieth-century missionary work has been the development of specialist missionary enterprises. The following are some of the major ones:

Health Care

Someone has said, 'God had only one Son and he was a medical missionary.' While this might be regarded as an extreme statement, healing the sick occupied much of our Lord's time and energy. When he sent out his disciples on evangelistic missions, he told them to 'preach the kingdom of God and to heal the sick'.[20] Many missionaries have done this to the best of their ability down through the ages, and missionaries trained in medicine, such as David Livingstone and Hudson Taylor, used medicine as an adjunct to evangelism. Specific medical programmes have been a feature of modern missionary endeavour since the latter part of the nineteenth century. By 1925, more than 2,000 missionary doctors and nurses were serving in mission hospitals and clinics throughout the world.

Perhaps the most notable medical missionary family is the Scudder family. In 1819 John Scudder left New York for Sri Lanka, and served in medical work for thirty-six years there and in India. 'In four generations, forty-two members of the Scudder family became missionaries, contributing well over a thousand combined years of missionary service.'[21] Many were doctors and the most well known was Ida Scudder who, in 1918, established the hospital and medical school in South India at Vellore. Two other famous medical missionaries of that era were Sir Wilfred Grenfell in Labrador and Albert Schweitzer in Africa.

Many highly skilled and dedicated women and men have served as medical missionaries, primarily in tropical countries. Some of them contributed much to the understanding and treatment of tropical diseases such as malaria and leprosy. Dr Paul Brand pioneered tendon transplant surgery for repairing hand and foot deformities in leprosy patients.[22] When I (John) was a medical student in London, meeting Paul Brand had an impact on my life. Some years later in Papua New Guinea in our hospital at Anguganak, leprosy treatment and control became an important part of our programme. Interest in medical missionary work was promoted widely in the 1950s and 1960s through Dr Paul White's *Jungle Doctor* series of books about Africa.

Mass Media

Radio Soon after commercial radio broadcasting began, far-sighted Christians saw the potential in using this medium to spread the gospel. By 1930 *The Lutheran Hour* was broadcasting the gospel over hundreds of stations worldwide. Radio can reach people in places where missionaries cannot go. Many thousands have come to know the Lord in Communist, Muslim and other countries, who would otherwise have never had a chance to hear the gospel. Churches have been started and nourished by means of regular support received via radio.

The world's first missionary radio programme was broadcast live in Spanish on Christmas Day, 1931, from HCJB (otherwise known as The Voice of the Andes) in Quito, Ecuador. From small beginnings with Clarence Jones, HCJB now broadcasts around the world in over a hundred languages and dialects twenty-four hours a day. They have ministries in over ninety countries, many of which also broadcast using local stations. Just after the Second World War, the Far East Broadcasting Company (FEBC) in Manila began. From here, the gospel is beamed into Asia and Russia in over forty languages. Evidence of the effectiveness of their programmes is revealed by the number of letters received from these countries. In one year, there were over 10,000 from China alone.

TransWorld Radio, set up by Paul Freed in 1954, is capable of reaching 80 per cent of the world's population from powerful transmitters in Monte Carlo, Swaziland, Cyprus, Sri Lanka and Guam. Some missions have added radio outreach to their other ministries, such as TEAM in Korea with HLKX, and SIM in Liberia with ELWA. Other groups are able to preach on local government or commercial radio stations. Various organisations in the homelands also help by producing quality programmes for use by missionary radio stations. To name two: LARE (Latin American Radio Evangelism), and CRC (Christian Resource Centre) in Christchurch, New Zealand. They produce hundreds of programmes a year, aimed at different audiences.

Television The medium of television is used extensively now, especially in America, to proclaim the gospel, mostly in English and aimed primarily at audiences at home. An increasing number of TV programmes are now being produced for cross-cultural mission use.

Records and audio tapes Another creative approach to spreading the gospel was born in 1939, when Joy Ridderhof, a missionary in Honduras was obliged to return home because of ill health. She started a work which became known as Gospel Recordings, producing short messages which were then recorded in various languages and made into records. These were then given to people in remote areas to listen to. The records were originally played on inexpensive, hand-turned gramophones. Now simple cassette playback machines that operate without batteries are used. Gospel messages have been recorded by native speakers in over 4,000 different languages and dialects, and many thousands of people have come to know the Lord though this means. A number of other organisations have been set up with a similar ministry.

Film and video The *Jesus* film, released in 1980 by Warner Brothers, is the one that has been used most extensively. In twenty years it has been seen by over two million people worldwide, and the dialogue has been translated into at least 550 languages. As a result of seeing the film or video, about 85 million people have shown interest or made decisions for Christ, and most have been followed up by local Christians. Many other evangelistic films and videos have been produced.

Bible Translation and Linguistics

Almost all the pioneer missionaries of the nineteenth century: William Carey, Robert Morrison, Adoniram Judson, Hudson Taylor, Henry Martyn and many others, were Bible translators. During that century, the Bible was translated as a whole or in part into about 500 languages. However, it was not until the twentieth century that the science of linguistics was more widely applied. In 1934 Cameron Townsend founded SIL (Summer Institute of Linguistics) and WBT (Wycliffe Bible Translators). Both organisations are concerned with training Bible translators and equipping missionaries with language learning skills, and now have a staff of over five thousand.

During the past century the Bible or portions of it have been translated into another 1,700 or so languages. Much of this work has been done by translators from the Bible Societies and other missions as well as Wycliffe. There are still about 2,000 other languages without a translation of the Bible. One brilliant linguist, teacher and author is Dr Kenneth Pike, who was President of SIL for thirty-four years. We were both fortunate enough to attend the first SIL course in England for three months in 1953 under the tutelage of Ken and Evelyn Pike. It was a significant part of our preparation for missionary service.

Literature

There is a still a tremendous dearth of Christian books and Bible commentaries in non-English languages, despite much work that has been done. The production of Christian literature has expanded rapidly in the last fifty years. Several organisations have been set up for this ministry, such as the Christian Literature Crusade, Operation Mobilisation (especially through their ships *Logos II* and *Doulos*, which are large travelling bookshops, among other things), World Literature Outreach, Evangelical Literature Overseas and Moody Literature Mission, to name a few.

Just as most of the New Testament was written by missionaries, so today many missionaries in different countries are involved in writing and producing literature to strengthen developing churches. The mission we worked with in Papua New Guinea (Christian Missions in Many Lands) saw this ministry as a priority. They invested money and personnel into

Christian Books Melanesia, in order to produce vital Christian literature, much of it in simplified English.

Teaching

If people can't read, there is not much point in translating the Bible or producing Christian literature for them. There is a felt need and huge demand for education in Third World countries, and many missionaries have been involved in basic education and literacy programmes, whether or not they were trained teachers. Many missions have developed effective schools at primary, secondary and tertiary levels. This has provided educated leadership for emerging churches, and in many instances, national and political leaders. Eventually, in most countries government education has caught up and taken over mission education. In some situations, Christian teachers have found it more strategic to work in national schools.

Theological education is an important area of teaching where missions are still having a vital input into the life of developing national churches, and this is happening in many countries. In Papua New Guinea, for example, the Christian Leaders' Training College has fed hundreds of graduates back into church leadership over the past thirty-five years.

Another avenue which has developed significantly more recently is teaching English as a second language. After a short course (TESL) even people who are not trained teachers can be equipped to do this work. There is a huge demand for learning English worldwide, and this presents opportunities for Christians to be effective witnesses in many countries, including those that are closed to any formal missionary activity.

Aviation

Prior to World War II a few missions operated small planes in their work. After the war, some Christian airmen in Britain,

America and Australia caught the vision of using their skills in missionary situations, and the Missionary Aviation Fellowship was born. The initiative for organised missionary aviation originated in Britain in 1945 with the New Zealanders, Murray Kendon and Trevor Strong. MAF today operates in thirty-five countries, with in excess of 180 light planes or helicopters, flown by highly skilled men and women pilots. Many other mission societies also have flight programmes. One of the largest is JAARS (Jungle Aviation and Radio Service) operated by Wycliffe. Missionary aviation has revolutionised the task of evangelising people in remote areas where other means of transport are difficult or even impossible, from tropical jungles to Arctic regions.

Our own mission hospital and the work of our missionary colleagues in Papua New Guinea owe much to the invaluable service provided by MAF. One of their pilots spotted an area of flat land beside a river in the centre of a relatively populated area of the Sepik Province, about one week's walk inland from Wewak. This eventually became the location for our hospital and medical programme, as well as a base mission centre.

Before that could happen, an airstrip had to be cut out of the jungle, using the help of men from surrounding villages. Once the trees had been removed and a five hundred yard strip levelled out, the ground was still not hard enough for the plane to land. So the missionary in charge of building the airstrip hit upon the idea of buying a football. When a hundred men started to kick the ball around, the ground was soon pounded down firmly!

Flying small planes in rugged mountainous areas with unpredictable weather changes can be very dangerous. It requires people with skill and courage, and there have been a number of air fatalities over the years in missionary aviation. One well-known missionary pilot was Nate Saint who died, not while flying, but at the hands of the Auca Indians, after he and four colleagues reached them by plane. Two of our personal friends who were pilots lost their lives in plane crashes in Papua New Guinea, Doug Hunt and John Harverson. One of our missionary families, Bob and Lois Wilkinson and their four children were killed, along with the pilot, in a plane crash while returning home from our annual mission conference.

Other Specialised Ministries

There are so many innovative aspects of missionary endeavour that it would be difficult to mention them all. We have referred to Amy Carmichael's work in rescuing children. Many orphanages and homes for handicapped children have been established by Christian missionaries. Other women have been led to work among prostitutes in the bigger cities of the world, providing them with hope, perhaps a home, and help to find alternative ways of making a living.

The twentieth century saw an epidemic of drug abuse, and some dedicated missionaries spend their lives working with drug addicts. Jackie Pullinger in Hong Kong is a wonderful example of someone committed to this ministry.[23] The AIDS epidemic throughout the world has led others to set up homes and hospices for victims. An organisation called Servants to the Asian Urban Poor works in the slums of big cities such as Manila, Bangkok and Phnom Penh. University students around the world are a significant target group for evangelism by IFES (International Fellowship of Evangelical Students), Campus Crusade for Christ and other organisations.

These are just some of the many and diverse ways missionaries are serving cross-cultural mission for the Lord today.

THE CHALLENGE OF MISSIONARY SERVICE TODAY

The task of missions is by no means complete. About one third of the earth's people call themselves Christians, one third are non-Christians living in already-reached people groups. One third of the world's population (2.1 billion persons) living in about 10,000 different people groups, are still considered 'unreached'. Less than 3 per cent of the 410,000 missionaries from all branches of Christendom work among them.[24]

Opportunities abound for people with almost any profession and skill to serve God overseas, in a variety of ways. The words of Jesus are as true today as ever they were:

'Look around you! Vast fields of human souls are ripening all around us, and are ready now for reaping. The reapers will be paid good wages and will be gathering eternal souls into the granaries of heaven!'[25]

Jesus said to his disciples on another occasion: 'The harvest is so great, and the workers are so few . . . Pray to the one in charge of harvesting, and ask him to recruit more workers for his harvest fields.'[26] In the very next verse we read that the disciples, who had been told to pray for workers to be raised up, were the first ones called to the task. The implications of this for us are hard to avoid.

The Call to Serve

It is important to define what we mean by 'a call' to serve. All Christians need a sense of call for whatever we do in life. This means that if we do not feel a conviction to serve Christ overseas, we should be convinced of a call to serve at home. The call or guidance that we all need is specific direction as to *where* we should serve. When Paul received a call to serve in

188

Macedonia rather than Asia, it was not a call to missionary service.[27] He was already a seasoned missionary, seven or eight years after being commissioned at Antioch. The call he received in a vision was to a people group; a call to a *location* not to a vocation.

However, to serve in overseas mission we do need a clear conviction that this is where God wants us. Otherwise we are more likely to be discouraged and deflected from the task when the going gets tough. God leads all of us in unique and different ways. We would like to share our own journeys and describe how we were led into missionary service.

Agnes My interest in missionary service came primarily through my family: parents, grandparents, aunts, uncles and cousins, all of whom had a passion for serving God. This influenced me from my early childhood. Two young cousins of mine had died in north China, and my aunt and uncle were left without children. I wondered if I could fill that gap and serve with them one day, but that dream never materialised.

As a teenager I read a number of missionary biographies. I also met many 'live missionaries', most of whom stayed in our home in the country. Having a year out with health problems gave me time for reflection, and perhaps it was not that I chose mission as an alternative to another career, but that it seemed the only option. One scripture that personally confirmed God's call to me was Isaiah 43:1–7.

With a desire to equip myself for service, I started nursing training at Christchurch Hospital in 1947. I had not previously contemplated a nursing career, but found it deeply satisfying, and I enjoyed the comradeship of other nurses who were also following the call of Christ. Nursing became my passion: to care for sick and suffering people in Christ's name. After general and maternity nursing training, I went to England where I trained in midwifery, and also did some studies at the

189

London Bible College. Eventually, when the way opened for the two of us to serve the Lord in Papua New Guinea, I set out confident that this was the culmination of the years of preparation.

John I was brought up in a missionary family, and my parents served in north China and Mongolia for a total of forty-three years. Dad's wife died in childbirth, leaving four young children, and later he married his wife's sister, who became my mother. She also died, a few days after I was born at the Peking University Medical College Hospital in 1929, and I was fostered by fellow missionaries. Three years later my father married again and I rejoined the family. From the age of seven I attended a mission boarding school at Chefoo, run by the CIM. These were lonely but happy years, and I am grateful for the good Christian education I received there, which encouraged me to make a personal commitment to Christ.

At the age of ten I developed bacterial endocarditis, for which there was no cure as those were pre-antibiotic days. My father travelled down from Mongolia aware that he might not even be in time for the funeral, but still believing God would heal me. So, together with some others, he anointed me with oil and prayed.[28] Immediately, my temperature dropped to normal and I began a process of recovery. This healing, as well as the dedication and encouragement of the doctor and nurse in the hospital (Dr Hallum and Mary Howie) sparked in me a desire to become a medical missionary one day.

In December 1941, when Japan entered the war by attacking the American fleet at Pearl Harbour, we were all interned by the Japanese. I was later transferred to a camp in Shanghai, then put on a repatriation ship headed for Lorenço Marques in Portuguese East Africa. There I met up with my parents again, whom I hadn't seen for two years, en route to

190

New Zealand. After the war, my parents returned to Mongolia and my father died in 1949 in the bitter winter of North West China, while attempting to flee from the Communists. Meanwhile, I worked my passage as a steward on a ship to London, with the purpose of studying medicine. I was greatly assisted in this goal by the Medical Missionary Association, who paid tuition fees and provided a hostel for students who were training for missionary work.

So my 'call' to missionary service was not through a vision or by some supernatural means, but became increasingly clear as I was aware of God's leading and provision. The harder part was discovering the location rather than the vocation. Agnes and I explored the needs and met with missionary doctors from many countries, without receiving any clear direction. Having become engaged in London, we returned to New Zealand to be married, and I completed two and a half years post-graduate training at Christchurch Hospital. At that time, Papua New Guinea was opening up to missionary work, and we joined with a team of young Brethren missionaries in the Sepik Province to set up a medical programme.

Just as a captain can't guide a ship when it's tied up at the wharf, so God is unlikely to guide anyone who isn't actively seeking to serve. We found that as we took one step in faith, God showed us the next.

The Cost of Service

Jesus actively discouraged people from following him who were not prepared for the cost involved.[29] There certainly are costs involved in serving as overseas missionaries, though they are not so great as in previous generations. In the nineteenth century it often took several months for missionaries to reach their destination, so there was no possibility of short rest breaks at home, and many never saw their homeland again. Because there were no vaccinations against such diseases as cholera, typhoid and rabies, or adequate treatment for malaria and amoebic infection, the majority of new missionaries died within the first year or two of arrival. The coast of West Africa became known as 'the white man's grave'. Even in the early part of the twentieth century, many missionary families experienced at least one death during their time abroad, as in our own family.

While health risks are much reduced now in most missionary situations, there are other sacrifices to be faced.[30] Obviously there is likely to be a lowered standard of living, but most missionaries are prepared to adopt a simple lifestyle and are not phased by this. Perhaps a harder one is the loss of professional status and ability to keep up in a way that would ensure a job if they have to return to the homeland. One thing we personally found hard was being dependent on others for financial support, when we had both been quite capable of earning our own living at home. The Lord had to deal with our pride. Future financial security and the chance to save for retirement are usually lost or reduced.

One significant cost is the sacrifice shared by the whole missionary family, when children have to be away at boarding school for extended periods. From a young age I (John) saw my parents briefly once a year. We found it a struggle to part with our own children for one term at a time in PNG. Children react differently to separation, and some find it harder than others.

But do MKs (missionary kids) suffer as a result of their experience? It depends largely on the attitude of the family and the degree of support they receive at school. Research reviewed in an article in *The Journal of Psychology and Christianity, 1986* showed that the typical MK had fewer psychological problems and rated higher academically than their USA counterparts.[31]

Our own children have shared with us some of their childhood pain from the separations, but clearly they gained a lot from their experiences. We thank God that they all love the Lord and have made a successful adjustment to life in New Zealand or Australia.

Another sacrifice many single women have faced is that their chances of marriage are significantly reduced by going to the missionfield. This step has not been taken without weighing up the cost. Some of them do eventually marry, but it has been estimated that about two thirds of overseas missionaries in the past century have been single women. This fact is not often mentioned in missionary histories.

There have been many missionary martyrs, from the first to the twentieth century. The Church worldwide is suffering greater persecution than ever before. It has been estimated there have been more Christians martyred in the last century than in the previous nineteen. 'Nearly two thirds of the world's population lives under regimes that still persecute Christians for their faith.'[32] This puts any sacrifices missionaries may make into perspective.

OPPORTUNITIES FOR OVERSEAS SERVICE TODAY

Long-term Missionary Work

There are still plenty of opportunities for full-time missionaries in many places. Effective church planting and the equipping of national leaders requires people who are prepared to learn the language and culture of the people thoroughly and stay for the long haul. 'Missionary usefulness increases with length of service by a kind of compound interest.'[33] Missionaries today work increasingly in partnership with the local churches, normally under the direction of national leadership.

To be an effective missionary requires some *specific training* at several levels. Spiritual preparation is obviously necessary in terms of a good grasp of Scripture and theology, usually obtained through a Bible College. Many colleges offer courses designed for missionary work. Training in spiritual formation is essential so that missionaries are able to meet the challenges of the spiritual warfare they are likely to encounter, as well as having the ability to nurture themselves spiritually in isolated situations. Some training in anthropology and linguistics is desirable for cross-cultural mission. There are some excellent books available about missionary training.[34]

Short-term Missionary Work

Over recent years more and more people have gone out to help in missionary situations for periods ranging from a few weeks to one or two years. They are usually people with specific skills in the building, medical, teaching or technical fields, which they can use without having to learn the language. However, it is still desirable for them to have some specific preparation and training before going in order to be really effective.

Many professions can be of help in this context, ranging from accountancy to youth work, with almost everything in between. Short-term workers can free missionaries to focus on church planting and other essential tasks. In our work in PNG the missionaries greatly appreciated such assistance, although it must be said that the care and supervision of short-term workers was sometimes distracting.

Such visits probably benefit the short-term worker as much as the missionary team. Many have caught the vision of working overseas and have returned later as long-term missionaries. Others who didn't return have become life-long mission supporters, generating interest in the home churches. Some missions organise parties of young people to visit their mission fields, and this has resulted in increased numbers of recruits. Others organise teams of young people to go to specific countries or cities and assist local churches with evangelistic outreach. Short-term mission ventures have been used in many enterprising ways, with varying degrees of success. It is important that the expectations of both the short-term workers and the missionaries on the field are clarified first.

'Finishers'

There is an awareness today of the potential for missionary service of older, mature Christians. They have been defined as 'Finishers', or 'second career missionaries'. These are people now coming into their fifties (known as the 'baby-boomer' generation, i.e. born between 1946–1964) who are free of family responsibilities and often financially independent. They have life experience, are at their peak professionally, have good health and a life expectancy of around twenty-five years. Research among this group has shown that just over 60 per cent of them would like to retire early to pursue a second career, and that they had at some stage considered missionary service, but for a variety of reasons never made it.[35]

A number of missions have been quick to integrate Finishers into their programme. There is a spectrum of opportunity open to people in this group, such as: finance, business administration, teaching, managing mission guest houses, teaching English, and many other situations which match their previous vocation and experience. Some become involved in the evangelisation and church planting programme, though this would usually entail language learning first.

Second-Time-Round Missionaries

Missionaries who have had to come home for family or health reasons, may be free later to make return visits to their previous field of service. Of course, this should be in partnership with, and at the invitation of, the national church leadership. Ex-missionaries can often contribute significantly to the work of the national church because of their past experience and knowledge of the language and culture. There are usually opportunities to teach the Scriptures and to come alongside and encourage local leaders. Some are able to make regular short visits which have been most effective, and others stay for longer periods.

Tentmakers

The term 'tentmakers' comes from the way Paul supported himself making tents at the same time as he worked as a missionary planting churches in Corinth and Thessalonica.[36] So 'tentmaker' has become a generic term for Christians who use their trade or profession overseas. They usually support themselves financially this way, though some of them are supported partially or fully from home.

Tentmakers are involved in missionary work where this is possible, or focus on friendship evangelism in 'limited access' or 'creative access' countries.[37] The only way Christians can enter many countries today is in a work capacity. Foreigners are often more accepted if they have employment as a valid reason for being there. It is significant that our Lord's last command to the Church was not to witness, but *to be* his witnesses,[38] which is essentially the role of Christian tentmakers in foreign countries.

The concept of 'tentmaking' is not new. In the eighteenth century the Moravian missionaries supported themselves with trades, which they taught to the national converts. William Carey took a job as manager of an indigo factory in India to support himself, and he encouraged other missionaries to be completely or partially self-supporting. There are many ways in which Christians today can use their profession and skills as self-supporting witnesses for Christ in other lands.

Opportunities in our Home Countries

Many thousands of people from Asia, Africa, South America, the Middle East, Pacific Islands and former Communist block countries come to western countries as tourists, students or immigrants. This provides a missionfield on our own doorstep, with wonderful opportunities to introduce people to Christ while they are away from their normal environment and cultural pressures. A number of returned missionaries have been able to continue a ministry with people from the land they worked in.

For any Christian, opportunities for effective 'overseas evangelism' abound through befriending immigrants and refugees, teaching them English, entertaining students or even providing accommodation for them. One couple who, for eleven years, have run a hostel for up to twenty foreign students told us,

Friendship with overseas students has been the most satisfying and productive Christian ministry we have been involved in. Each student, with their distinctive personality, becomes our personal friend. Some become Christians while with us and then return home as witnesses to family and friends. Others are not so quick to respond, but will never forget their overseas Christian encounter.[39]

A number of missions, such as Interserve and OMF, have full-time mission partners working with ethnic minority groups living in big cities in Europe and North America. National churches send missionaries to work with their own people who have migrated overseas, such as the Chinese Christian Overseas

Mission, who have an effective ministry with Chinese expatriates all over Europe. The modern world has been described as a 'global village', and so cross-cultural mission is to people-groups with identifiable need, regardless of location.[40]

Member Care

One of the most neglected groups in the arena of missionary endeavour has been the missionaries themselves. Some missions provide good support and pastoral care for their workers, but other groups do not address this very well. Missionary life can be lonely, discouraging and spiritually draining. One of the most damaging factors (and the one that causes the most missionary attrition) is inter-personal conflict and relationship breakdown among missionaries. Missionaries are only human, and working together in a team with strong-minded people, whom you might not even choose as friends back home, calls for a lot of grace, humility and good communication.

Some missions provide pastoral visits to the field from home mission staff. This is good, but has the problem of the carer/counsellor being someone in a position of authority. A growing number of people today, who are independent of any mission organisation, are making themselves available for pastoral care visits to missionaries on location. Joyce and David Huggett have been offering spiritual retreats for groups of missionaries on the field (especially in the Middle East) as well as at home.[41] We have been involved in this ministry in a small way over the past few years, and were invited to visit groups of missionaries in Mongolia, Afghanistan, Thailand, Vietnam, Ecuador and Papua New Guinea for periods of three to four weeks. In these locations we ran retreats and seminars and spent time with individuals or couples, discussing spiritual, emotional and medical issues.

Care of Missionaries From the Home Base

This is another important aspect of missionary support. There is a lot that churches can do to support their missionaries on the field. This includes prayer, financial and logistic support, regular communication by letter or e-mail, the provision of technical assistance in specialised fields while they are away. During home leave there are practical matters such as the need of a vehicle or accommodation. Returning missionaries also need practical support in the 're-entry' process back to their homeland.[42]

Over the past seven years we have been part of a team running Missionary Enrichment Retreats twice a year in New Zealand, which focus on the worker, rather than the work. These retreats last about a week and provide not only time for spiritual renewal, but an opportunity to look at issues like: burnout prevention, communication, conflict resolution, working as a team, spiritual warfare. One-to-one counselling is also available for those who want to deal with personal issues.

SUMMARY

In this chapter we have attempted to cover a brief history of Christian missions and an overview of missionary activity today. While much has been done, the task is far from complete. Adoniram Judson said, 'Our responsibility is not to bring the whole world to Christ, but to bring Christ to the whole world.'[43] It is impossible to avoid the conclusion that every committed Christian has a role to play in some way in overseas mission. 'The church exists by mission as fire exists by burning.'[44]

REFLECTIONS AND EXERCISES

1. HISTORY   Describe your reactions to reading this brief record of missionary endeavour over the past twenty centuries? What have you learned?
- Discuss this together in your small group.
- Determine to read at least one missionary biography. You'll be blessed!

2. THE CALL   Have you ever felt challenged to serve God overseas?

   If so, what steps have you taken to verify this call and to act on it?

   Review the section on 'Opportunities for overseas service today.'

   If not, do you feel a sense of call to stay where you are in the job you have?
- It would be helpful to write about this in your journal, or to share it in your small group or with a close friend.

3. THE COST   If you are thinking of serving God overseas, have you thought through the sacrifices that might be involved?
- How seriously have you considered training for cross-cultural mission?

4. OPPORTUNITIES AT HOME   Have you considered the possibilities of befriending students or immigrants from other countries with a view to sharing your faith? Think about opportunities in your locality.
- In what ways could you be involved in the support of missionaries overseas, perhaps from your own church? How about writing to a missionary, and making a commitment to pray for him or her regularly?

Conclusion

Service is a choice we all face:

> we either serve ourselves or others;
> we serve sin or righteousness;
> we serve our own desires or serve God.

Other-centred service is a satisfying way of life. When service becomes celebration we are free to enjoy life to the full. Albert Schweitzer once said: 'I don't know what your destiny will be. One thing I do know is that the ones among you who will be truly happy are those who have sought and found how to serve.'

We have looked at some of the many ways the principle of service affects the whole of life: our family, friendships, work and our relationship with God. The Bible provides us not only with instructions on how to serve, but gives us models of true service – primarily seen in the life of Jesus, the Servant King. The Scriptures are saturated with the concept, and service is central to the Christian life. Service is the Christian's vocation and God has provided us with the Holy Spirit to strengthen and guide our service.

Opportunities for service abound. We have identified some of the many ways to serve: at home, at work, at church, in our community and overseas. We only need to open our eyes and look around us, and Jesus told us to do just that: 'I tell you, open your eyes and look at the fields! They are ripe for harvest!'[1] He is wanting servants to work in his harvest field, but the biggest problem God has with his servants is absenteeism.

Just as athletes who succeed have spent years in training, so servants need to be trained and equipped for the task. As we grow in character so we become more equipped for service. In discovering our unique personality and gifting we are more aware of the tools God has given us. These abilities need to be honed and developed so that we can serve effectively. It is also essential for servants to be continually nourished as we learn how to nurture ourselves physically, intellectually, emotionally, socially and spiritually. This is the way to maintain our effectiveness.

We do not serve in order to receive rewards but out of a love for God and for others. However, our Father God lovingly rewards the service of his children in many ways: physically, emotionally and spiritually. As was pointed out earlier, our greatest reward is God himself, when we become his children, his servants/slaves and his friends. The joy of giving ourselves and our resources to God's service is unsurpassed, and having a share in what he is doing in his world is an amazing privilege. The pleasure of seeing 'fruit' in the lives of others as a result of our service is rewarding but hard to measure – whether the 'fruit' is their spiritual growth, an ability to overcome personal problems, the enjoyment of a better living situation or recovery from illness.

Much of the benefit of being a servant is one's *personal growth* towards maturity and wholeness. Being a servant teaches us how to follow Christ in real terms. In setting out for Papua New Guinea, we dreamed of changing the world! The reality was we were changed, though hopefully we were able to help others along the way. Two of our medical friends expressed it this way: 'Seeing my work with patients as an opportunity to serve others freed me from the tyranny of self.' 'A medical career was wonderful therapy for me. It brought me in touch with the real world in all its suffering and pain. I had to face up to the biblical view of life, and my faith became alive as a result.'[2]

The forms of service we are led into do not matter much. The important thing is *how* we serve and *whom* we serve. Two Jewish writers, a thousand years apart, expressed it this way: 'Whatever your hand finds to do, do it with all your might.' and 'Whatever you do, do it all for the glory of God.'[3]

Outstanding human achievements are remembered for a generation or two, and some of them may even be recorded in the annals of history. Humble service is seldom noticed by people, but it is what God is looking for.

What a celebration it will be one day, to see Jesus face-to-face and hear him say, 'Well done, good and faithful servant!'[4]

Notes and References

Prequel
1. John 10:10.
2. *Created for Love* (Guildford: Eagle, 1994).
   Created for Intimacy (Guildford: Eagle, 1996).
   Created to be Whole (Guildford: Eagle, 1998).
3. 1 Peter 2:16.

Chapter One: The Crisis of Service
1. Sir Wilfred Grenfell, pioneer English medical missionary to Labrador. He trained at the same hospital that I (John) did in London (The Royal London) and provided part of my inspiration for becoming a medical missionary.
2. 2 Peter 2:19 (TLB). See also John 8:34,35; Romans 6:15–22.
3. Matthew 22:37–40.
4. William Temple, *Christianity and Social Order* (New York: Seabury, 1977).
5. Philippians 2:4; see also 1 Corinthians 10:24.
6. Luke 6:38.
7. 2 Corinthians 9:6.
8. Proverbs 11:24, 25 (TLB); see also Isaiah 58:10, 11.
9. Matthew 6:19–21 (The Message).
10. 2 Corinthians 8:7; see also: Malachi 3:8–11; 2 Corinthians 8:2–15; 9:6–11; Galatians 6:6.
11. Richard Gillard, *Brother, let me be your servant* (London: Scripture in Song, 1977) Vol. II, No 51.
12. C.S.Lewis, *The Four Loves* (London: Fount, 1960).
13. See 1 John 4:7–8, 19.
14. John Powell, *Unconditional Love* (Illinois: Argus, 1978) p 70.
15. Matthew 6:3.
16. Galatians 5:13.
17. Romans 7:14–25.
18. Matthew 6:24..
19. 2 Corinthians5:14.
20. Acts 20:19.
21. Ephesians 6:7; Colossians 3:22–24.
22. K. Singh, *Gurus, God Men and Good People* (New Delhi: Orient Longman, 1975) p 119.
23. A helpful book on this topic is: *Church: Why Bother?* by Philip Yancey (Grand Rapids: Zondervan, 1998).
24. Colossians 1:25.
25. 1 Corinthians 3:6–17.
26. 1 Corinthians 12:12–27.
27. Dietrich Bonhoeffer, *Life Together* (London: SCM, 1954).
28. 1 Corinthians 12:26.
29. Michael Green, *Freed to Serve: Training and Equipping for Ministry* (London: Hodder & Stoughton, 1988) p 10.
30. Ibid., p 26.
31. Acts 4:27; Isaiah 42:1; Matthew 12:18. See Chapter Three for a further study on the biblical concept of servanthood.
32. Matthew 10:42.
33. Matthew 25:35,36.

204

34. Matthew 25:31–46.
35. Proverbs 25:21.
36. Hannah Whitall Smith, *The Christian's Secret of a Happy Life* (London: James Nisbet, 1896) p 186.
37. Wayne Oates, *Confessions of a Workaholic* (Nashville: Abingdon, 1971).
38. This is explored further in *Created for Love*, op. cit., pp 68ff.
39. Mark 9:33–37.
40. Mark 10:35–45 (emphasis ours).
41. Luke 22:24–27.
42. John 13:2–7.
43. Romans 12:2; Ephesians 4:23.
44. Hannah Smith, op. cit. p 190.

Chapter Two: Lifestyle Service

1. '*Ich dien*' is the German motto on the coat of arms of the Prince of Wales.
2. See L. Peplau and D. Pelman (Editors) *Loneliness: A Sourcebook of Current Theory and Therapy* (New York: John Wiley & Sons, 1982). A valuable overview on research and literature on loneliness.
3. John and Agnes Sturt, *Created for Intimacy* (Guildford: Eagle, 1996) p 26.
4. Aristotle, 384–322 BC, *Nichomachean Ethics*, Book viii, Sec 1.
5. C.S. Lewis, *The Four Loves* (London: Fount, 1960).
6. J. & A. Sturt, op. cit.
7. Luke 14:12–14.
8. Matthew 25:35.
9. Hebrews 13:2.
10. Proverbs 15:17.
11. Luke 7:36–50; 14:1–6.
12. Luke 10:38; John 12:1–4.
13. Luke 22:19.
14. Matthew 26:20–25; Mark 14:18–21; Luke 22:21–23; John 13:21–30, Psalm 41:9.
15. Revelation 3:20.
16. Henri Nouwen, *Reaching Out* (London: Font Paperbacks, 1980) pp 68,69.
17. John 13:34,35.
18. Proverbs 22:6.
19. Kahlil Gibran, *The Prophet* (London: Heinemann, 1972) pp 20, 21. Gibran (1883–1931) was a Lebanese-American Christian poet, artist and philosopher who wrote extensively in English and Arabic.
20. Psalm 127:3,4.
21. 1 Timothy 5:8 (emphsis ours).
22. Matthew 19:27–29.
23. Luke 9:48 (TLB).
24. 2 Corinthians 1:3b, 4.
25. Matthew 10:8; Mark 3:15 (AV); Luke 10:9.
26. 1 Corinthians 4:5.
27. Galatians 6:2–5.
28. John 13:34; 15:12; Matthew 22:39.
29. The Good News Bible renders it: 'help to carry'; The Living Bible: 'share'.
30. For a comprehensive review of 'Compassion Fatigue' (secondary traumatic stress disorder) see *Compassion Fatigue*, edited by Charles Figley (New York: Brunner/ Mazel, 1995).
31. David Augsburger, *Pastoral Counselling Across Cultures* (Philadelphia: West-minster Press, 1986) pp 368ff.

32. Henri Nouwen, *The Wounded Healer* (New York, Doubleday, Image Books, 1979) p 88.

33. Ibid. p 72.

34. Diagram adapted from D. Augsburger, op. cit. p 369.

35. Luke 7:50; 8:48; 17:19 (emphasis ours).

36. D. Augsburger, op. cit. p 371.

37. Isaiah 53:5 (emphasis ours).

38. James Houston, *Prayer: The Transforming Friendship* (Oxford: Lion, 1993) p 159.

39. Ephesians 6:19.

40. Romans 8:26,27; Ephesians 6:18.

41. Ephesians 3:20.

42. Ephesians 6:18 (Contemporary English Version).

43. Margaret Magdalen, *Jesus – Man of Prayer* (London: Hodder & Stoughton, 1993) p 107.

Chapter Three: Biblical Basis for Service

1. Galatians 5:13.

2. Genesis 2:2. See also Exodus 31:17 '. . . on the seventh day [God] rested, and was refreshed' (literally: 'refreshed himself').

3. Genesis 2:15 (emphasis ours).

4. Genesis 4:19–22.

5. Exodus 31:2–5; 35:30–35.

6. Here are a few of the references where work is ascribed to God:

   a) *Creator*: creation is the 'work of his hands' – Psalm 8:3; 19:1; 95:5.

   b) *Shepherd*: Psalm 23; 80:1; Isaiah 40:11; Jeremiah 31:10; Micah 2:12; Zechariah 13:7–9; John 10:11.

   c) *Architect/builder*: Psalm 118:22,23; Isaiah 28:16,17; 54:11,12.

   d) *Potter*: Job 10:8,9; Isaiah 45:9; Jeremiah 18:6; Romans 9:20,21.

   e) *Tailor*: Genesis 3:21; Psalm 30:11; Isaiah 61:10; Exekiel 16:10.

   f) *Gardener and Orchardist*: Genesis 2:8,9; Ezekiel 31:8,9; Mark 12: 1–11; John 15:1.

   Some excellent books that explore the concept of work are:

   a) Robert Banks, *God the Worker* (Sydney: Albatross, 1992).

   b) Leland Ryken, *Work and Leisure* (Leicester: IVP, 1989).

   c) John McInnes, *The New Pilgrims* (Sydney: Albatross, 1980), Chapter 7.

   d) Alan Richardson, *The Biblical Doctrine of Work* (London: SCM, 1952).

7. Psalm 127:1.

8. 2 Corinthians 6:1.

9. John 4:34; 5:17.

10. Acts 18:3; 1 Corinthians 4:12; 9:6; 2 Thessalonians 3:7,8. The practice of 'tentmaking' is explored further in Chapter Seven.

11. 1 Thessalonians 4:11; Ephesians 4:28.

12. Titus 3:1 (RSV).

13. 1 Corinthians 10:31; see also Ecclesiastes 9:10; Colossians 3:23, 24.

14. Matthew 25:14–30.

15. Ryken, op. cit. p 152.

16. Exodus 3:12.

17. Exodus 9:1.

18. Romans 9:4; Hebrews 8:5; 9:1,6.

19. Romans 12:1.

20. Acts 13:2; Romans 15:16,27; 2 Corinthians 9:12; Philippians 2:17,25,30.

21. Thomas Kelly, *A Testament of Devotion* (New York: Harper & Row, 1941) pp 32,33. Thomas Kelly (1893–1941) was a Quaker pastor from Ohio, who in later years taught philosophy at Harvard University.

22. Brother Lawrence, *The Practice of the Presence of God* .Translated by J. Delaney (New York: Doubleday, 1977). Brother Lawrence (1611–1691) was a lay brother in a barefoot Carmelite order in Paris. He had no formal education but left a profound spiritual legacy. After his death his letters and conversations were compiled in a book by his abbot, Joseph de Beaufort.
23. Horatius Bonar (1808–1889) was a minister in the Presbyterian and later the Free Church of Scotland, who wrote the words for 660 hymns.
24. Michael Green, *Freed to Serve* (London: Hodder & Stoughton, 1988) p 22.
25. Luke 24:21; Acts 1:6.
26. Mark 10: 42–45 (emphasis ours).
27. Isaiah 42:1–4; Matthew 12:18–21.
28. Philippians 2:5–8.
29. John 6:38; see also Romans 15:3; Hebrews 10:7.
30. Matthew 9:36; 14:14; 15:32; 20:34; Mark 1:41; 6:34; 8:2; Luke 7:13.
31. John 19:25–27; Luke 23:28–43.
32. Isaiah 52:13–53:11 (emphasis ours).
33. Luke 22:24; Matthew 18:1; Mark 9:34; Luke 9:46.
34. John 13:1–17.
35. 1 Peter 5:2–6.
36. John 13:15.
37. Luke 12:35–48.
38. This is the message of our book, *Created for Love* (Guildford: Eagle, 1994).
39. John 21:1–23.
40. Matthew 4:18,19; Mark 1:16,17.
41. J. Kise, D. Stark, S. Hirsh, *Life Keys* (Minneapolis: Bethany House, 1996) p 222.
42. 2 Corinthians 12:9,10.
43. Romans 1:1; Philippians 1:1; Titus 1:1; James 1:1; 2 Peter 1:1; Jude 1.
44. John 7:5; Mark 3:21.
45. Revelation 1:1; 15:3.
46. 1 Corinthians 9:19 (emphasis ours); see also 2 Corinthians 4:5.
47. Colossians 1:7; 4:7,12.
48. 1 Corinthians 4:1.
49. 1 Peter 2:16.
50. Murray Harris, *Slave of Christ* (Leicester: InterVarsity Press, 1999) p 25.
51. Ibid., p 34 for details.
52. 1 Peter 1:18,19; 1 Corinthians 7:23.
53. *The Book of Common Prayer* (1662) Collect for Peace in Morning Prayer.
54. 1 Corinthians 6:20.
55. Hebrews 2:14,15.
56. Galatians 5:13.
57. 2 Peter 2:17–19.
58. Martin Luther, *Christian Liberty* (Philadelphia: Muhlenberg, 1943) p 5.
59. 2 Corinthians 1:22; 5:5; Ephesians 1:13,14.
60. Acts 2:18; Joel 2:28,29.
61. Galatians 5:13,16.
62. Gene Getz, *Serving One Another* (Wheaton: Victor Books, 1984) p 36.
63. Galatians 5:22,23.
64. 2 Timothy 2:24 (Good News Bible).
65. 1 Peter 5:5; see also Romans 12:3; James 4:6.
66. Philippians 2:7,8.
67. Matthew 11:29.

68. Acts 20:19; Ephesians 4:2; see also 2 Corinthians 10:1; Titus 3:2.
69. Colossians 1:20.
70. Matthew 5:9 (Good News Bible).
71. Matthew 5:7 (Good News Bible).
72. Galatians 5:22.
73. John 1:14.
74. Colossians 1:7; 4:7; also Ephesians 6:21.
75. 1 Corinthians 4:2 (KJV).
76. Matthew 25:14–30.
77. Matthew 5:14.
78. Charles Swindoll, *Improving Your Serve* (London: Hodder & Stoughton, 1983) p 136.
79. 1 John 3:1–2.
80. John 15:15.
81. Revelation 22:3,4.
82. Matthew 25:21–23.
83. Romans 1:9.
84. Richard Foster, *Celebration of Discipline* (London: Hodder & Stoughton, 1983) p 122.

Chapter Four: Equipped for Service
1.   2 Timothy 3:17 (Good News Bible).
2.   Exodus 4:1–20.
3.   Henri Nouwen, *Letters to Marc* (London: Darton, Longman & Todd, 1988) p 1.
4.   The concept of self-esteem is explored more fully in our book, *Created for Love* (Guildford: Eagle, 1994).
5.   Matthew 22:39; Galatians 5:14; James 2:8.
6.   Philippians 2:3,4.
7.   Philippians 1:21; 2 Corinthians 5:14.
8.   John 21:15–17.
9.   Mark 4:38; John 4:4ff.
10. We develop this concept in *Created to be Whole* (Guildford: Eagle, 1998).
11. a) H. Cloud and J. Townsend, *Boundaries: When to Say No, When to Say Yes, to Take Control of Your Life* (Grand Rapids: Zondervan, 1996).
     b) *Boundaries with Kids* (Grand Rapids: Zondervan, 1998).
     c) *Boundaries in Marriage* (Grand Rapids: Zondervan, 1999).
12. Mark 1:36–38.
13. Matthew 4:5–7; 12:38, 39; 27:41–44.
14. Carl Jung, *Psychological Types* (Princeton, NJ: University Press, 1923).
15. Isabel Myers, *Gifts Differing* (Oxford: Oxford Psychological Press, 1990).
16. a) Isabel Myers, et al., *MBTI Manual*, 3rd ed (Palo Alto, Consulting Psycho-logical Press, 1998).
     b) M. Goldsmith and M. Wharton, *Knowing Me, Knowing You* (London: SPCK, 1993) a simpler description of personality type and the relationship between type and personality.
17. Understanding the dynamics of Type in relationships is well explained in *16 Ways to Love Your Lover* by O. Kroeger and M. Thuesen (New York: Bantam Doubleday Dell, 1994).
18. O. Kroeger and J. Thuesen, *Type Talk at Work* (New York: Bantam Doubleday Dell, 1992). See also *MBTI Manual*, op. cit., Chapter 12.
19. Dag Hammerskjöld, *Markings* (London: Faber, 1966).
20. D. Keirsey and M. Bates, *Please Understand Me* (Del Mar: Prometheus Nemesis, 1984).
21. R. Taylor and L. Morrison, *Taylor-Johnson Temperament Manual* (Los Angeles: Psychological Publications, 1984).
22. Galatians 5:22, 23.
23. Ephesians 4:12 (emphasis ours).

24. 1 Peter 4:10 (emphasis ours). See also v 11.
25. B. Bugbee, D. Cousins, B. Hybels, *Network: The Right People in the Right Places for the Right Reasons* (Grand Rapids: Zondervan, 1994).
26. 1 Timothy 4:14.
27. Matthew 25:24–30.
28. John Bunyan (1628–1688), *Grace Abounding to the Chief of Sinners* (Chicago: Moody Bible Institute Press, 1959).
29. Our book *Created to be Whole,* op. cit., deals with effective ways of preventing burnout.
30. 1 Corinthians 3:16; 2 Corinthians 6:16.
31. John 8:28.
32. 2 Corinthians 12:9,10; see also Hebrews 11:34.
33. 2 Timothy 3:17 (GNB, emphasis ours).
34. Psalm 119:19,20 (TLB).
35. Joshua 1:8; Psalm 1:2; 119:97.
36. Psalm 119:99.
37. Mark 1:35; 6:46.
38. Henri Nouwen, *The Way of the Heart* (London: Daybreak, 1987) p 26.
39. Some helpful books on prayer are:
    a) Joyce Huggett, *Learning the Language of Prayer* (Oxford: BRF, 1994).
    b) Richard Foster, *Prayer: Finding the Heart's True Home* (London: Hodder & Stoughton, 1992).
    c) James Houston, *Prayer, the Transforming Friendship* (Oxford: Lion Publishing, 1993).
40. Luke 11:1.
41. Ephesians 5:18.
42. Acts 6:3.
43. Acts 2:4; 4:8, 31; 6:5; 7:55; 9:17; 11:24; 13:9.
44. Luke 4:1, 14, 18; 10:21; Acts 1:2, 10:38.
45. Hebrews 9:14; Romans 8:11.
46. Henri Nouwen in his introduction to *Soul Friend: An Invitation to Spiritual Direction,* by Kenneth Leech (London: DLT, 1994).
    Some other useful books on Spiritual Direction:
    a) Margaret Guenther, *Holy Listening: The Art of Spiritual Direction* (London, DLT, 1992).
    b) Eugene Peterson, *The Contemplative Pastor: Returning to the Art of Spiritual Direction* (Grand Rapids: Eerdmans, 1989).
47. J. Smith, R. Foster, *A Spiritual Formation Workbook* (San Francisco: Harper, 1991). This book gives a clear description of how to run a Renovaré group and a guide to cover eight sessions, by which time a new group would be well established.
48. Henri Nouwen, *Reaching Out* (London: Fount Paperbacks, 1980) p 100.

Chapter Five: Rewards of Service

1. Seneca, Lucius Annaeus, 4 BC to AD 65. Roman philosopher, writer and statesman. (*Epistulae ad Lucium,* 18, sec 20.)
2. Aesop is the name traditionally given to the author of a collection of Greek fables, which were put together about the 4th century BC.
3. Ignatius Loyola, 1491–1556, Spanish theologian, founder of the Jesuits.
4. Luke 17:10.
5. Genesis 15:1.
6. James 2:23.
7. Genesis chapter 18.
8. Genesis 15:6; Romans 4:3; Galatians 3:6; James 2:23; see also Hebrews 11:8–12.
9. Hebrews 11:6 (emphasis ours).

10. J.S. House, K.R. Landis, D. Umberson, 'Social Relationships and Health' (*Science*, 1988 Vol 241, 540–545).
11. Dr James Lynch, *The Broken Heart* (New York: Basic Books, 1979).
12. A. Kohn, 'Beyond Selfishness' (*Psychology Today*, October 1988, 34–38).
13. Acts 20:35 (NIV and GNB).
14. William Barclay, *The Gospel of Matthew, Vol 1* (Edinburgh: St Andrew Press, 1958) p 84.
15. John Haggai, *Paul J. Meyer and the Art of Giving* (Atlanta: Kobrey Press, 1994) p 146.
16. A. Luks, 'Helper's High' (*Psychology Today*, October 1988, 39–42).
17. Thomas Hobbes, 1588–1694, controversial political philosopher and writer.
18. Matthew 22:39; see also Leviticus 19:18; Galatians 5:14.
19. 1 John 4:20; James 2:14–18.
20. Romans 12:5 (TLB, emphasis ours). See also 1 Corinthians 12:12–30; Ephesians 1:23; 2:16; 3:6; 3:4, 12, 16; 5:30; Colossians 1:18; 2:19; 3:15.
21. Matthew 5:13; 13:33.
22. Richard Foster, *Celebration of Discipline* (London, Hodder & Stoughton, 1983) p 113.
23. John 15:8.
24. John 15:4–7.
25. Galatians 5:22,23.
26. Colossians 1:10 (emphasis ours).
27. Luke 15:7,10.
28. 1 Thessalonians 2:19,20.
29. Michael Griffiths, *Tinker, Tailor, Missionary?* (Leicester: IVF/OM Press, 1993) p 133.
30. Luke 10:20.
31. Hebrews 11:13,39 (emphasis ours).
32. 1 Corinthians 3:7–9 (emphasis ours).
33. Revelation 22:12.
34. Matthew 5:12.
35. 2 Corinthians 5:10; see also Romans 14:10.
36. Matthew 25:31–33; see also Revelation 20:11. (Some commentators believe that these references refer to different occasions.)
37. W.E. Vine, *A Comprehensive Dictionary of the Original Greek Words with their Precise Meanings for English Readers* (Virginia: Macdonald Publishing) p 622.
38. 1 Corinthians 3:14,15.
39. C.L. Blomberg, *Interpreting the Parables* (Downer Grove: InterVarsity, 1990) p 224.
40. Matthew 20:1–16.
41. Luke 23:42,43.
42. Genesis 18:25.
43. 1 Corinthians 9:25–27.
44. 2 Timothy 4:8; see also Proverbs 11:18.
45. James 1:12; Revelation 2:10.
46. 1 Thessalonians 2:19.
47. 1 Peter 5:4.
48. 1 Corinthians 15:58.
49. Matthew 25:21,23.
50. George Eliot, *Daniel Deronda*, Bk vi, Ch 46.
51. Revelation 22:3,4 (emphasis ours).

Chapter Six: Specialised Service
1. S. Covey & R. Merrill, *First Things First* (New York: Simon & Schuster, 1994) p 291.
2. The following people (not acknowledged within the text) were interviewed regarding their views on the service aspect of their profession:

a) *Nursing:* Megan Clemow, Margaret Corin, Daphne Dewerse, Gwyneth Peat, Eileen Taylor, Robyn Yule.

b) *Medicine:* Alan Fraser, Beryl Howie, Ken Mickleson, Brian and Sue Parry (specialist physicians or surgeons); Alan Broom, Barbara Fraser, Sarah Rishworth (family doctors).

c) *Counselling/psychotherapy:* Richard Charmley, Roger Elley-Brown, John McAlpine, Margaret Mourant.

d) *Social work:* Graeme Bruges, Mark Darling, Peter Hepburn, Elaine McFadzean, Alfred and Moka Ngaro.

e) *Teaching:* – *Primary:* Russell Burt, Sheila Mickleson, Glenys Yeoman,

– *Secondary:* Margaret Elley-Brown, Jocelyn Grantham, Margaret Mourant, Warren Peat, Robin Staples, Dennis Thorp.

– *Tertiary:* Dr John Hitchen (Theology), Dr Peter Lineham (History), Professor Brian Parry (Surgery), Dr Sue Parry (Physician).

f) *Law:* Warren Brookbanks, Richard Browning, David Burt, Andrew Clemow, Jillian Guptill, Steve McFadzean, Paul Rishworth.

g) *Business:* Dick Hubbard.

h) *Writing:* Julie Belding (President of NZ Christian Writers Guild), Joyce Huggett, Margaret Mourant.

i) *Literature promotion:* David Wavre (publisher); Malcolm Frith, Mike   Hadwin, Paul Humphries, John McConnell, (booksellers).
3. Nancy Hardesty, *Great Women of Faith* (Grand Rapids: Baker, 1980) p 104.
4. D.C. Lortie, *Schoolteacher: A Sociological Study* (Chicago: University of   Chicago Press, 1975).
5. W. Baver, *A Greek–English Lexicon of the New Testament*, 2nd Edition, (Chicago: Chicago University Press) p 618.
6. 1 John 2:1 (KJV, 'advocate'); John 14:16 (KJV 'Paraklete, Comforter; NIV, Counsellor)
7. Satan is the 'accuser' – Revelation 12:10; God is the 'Judge' – Acts 17:31; Hebrews 12:23.
8. Proverbs 31:8–9 (GNB).
9. Robert Laidlaw, 1885–1970. He wrote the well-known Gospel Tract, *The Reason Why*, of which about 25 million copies have been printed in over 30 languages. He wrote it originally as a means of sharing his faith with his staff.
10. Ian Hunter, Robert Laidlaw, *Man for our Time* (Auckland: Castle, 1999) pp 73, 76.
11. Ibid., p 298.
12. Ibid., pp 23, 283.
13. Psalm 82:3.
14. Deuteronomy 15:11.
15. Proverbs 19:17.
16. Luke 4:18,19.
17. Luke 7:22.
18. Statistics from the United Nations Human Development Report, 1997.
19. Ronald Sider, *Rich Christians in an Age of Hunger* (London: Hodder Stoughton, 1979).
20. See Acts 11:27–29; 24:17; 1 Corinthians 16:1–4; 2 Corinthians 8:19–21.
21. OECD, Voluntary Aid for Development: The Role of NGOs (Paris: OECD, 1988) p 18.
22. D.C. Korten, *Getting to the 21st Century: Voluntary Action and the Global Agenda* (Hartford: Kumarian Press, 1990) p 1.
23. Ibid., pp 114–123.
24. *Auckland Community Resource Directory* (Auckland: Life Line, 1999).
25. 1 Peter 2:5,9; Hebrews 13:15.
26. Ephesians 4:12.
27. 1 Peter 4:10.
28. 1 Corinthians 12:27.

29. W.H. Brackney, *Christian Voluntarism: Theology and Praxis* (Grand Rapids: Eerdmans, 1997) p 129.
30. This aspect has been explored well by others, see:
   Michael Griffiths, *Get Your Act Together, Cinderella* (Leicester: IVP/STL,1989) Ch 9.
   Tinker, Tailor, Missionary? (Leicester: IVP/OM, 1992) Ch 10.
   Jerry White, *The Church and Parachurch: An Uneasy Marriage* (Portland: Multnomah, 1983).
31. An exciting book which gives an insight into the work of World Vision is by Graham Irvine, *Best Things in the Worst Times* (Wilsonville: Book Partners, 1996).
32. Information and comments provided by Peter Sutcliffe (PMI Auckland); Dr Peter Lineham; Colin and Agnes Broughton (PMI Christchurch); Stephen and Margaret Young (Prison Chaplain, Tongariro Prison), Ian Elliott (PFI Regional Representative for the Pacific).
33. Charles Colson, *Born Again* (London: Hodder & Stoughton, 1976).
34. Isaiah 42:3.
35. This aspect of restorative justice is explored well in the book *Convicted* by Charles Colson and Peter Timms (Cambridge: Crossway, 1992).
36. Luke 4:18.
37. Matthew 25:36.

Chapter Seven: Cross-Cultural Mission Service

1. Jim Elliott, missionary to the Auca Indians, martyred in 1956.
2. Genesis 12:3; Psalm 67.
3. Acts 1:8.
4. Calculated from statistics supplied by David Barrett & Todd Johnson, *International Bulletin of Missionary Research,* Vol 32:1, January 1999.
5. Acts 8:1–4; 11:19.
6. Acts 11:20,21.
7. Barrett & Johnson, op. cit., p 24.
8. Resources used for this section included:
   Stephen Neill, *A History of Christian Missions* (Harmondsworth: Pelican,1964).
   Ruth Tucker, *From Jerusalem to Irian Jaya* (Grand Rapids: Zondervan Academic, 1983).
   D. Winter & S. Hawthorne, Eds, *Perspectives on the World Christian Movement* (Pasadena: William Carey Library, 1981).
9. John 4:28–42.
10. Acts 8:4–25.
11. Acts 13:1–4.
12. Eusebius, *Ecclesiastical History III*, 37, 2–3.
13. Stephen Neill, op. cit., pp 38,39.
14. Professor Latourette (1884–1968) premier Christian historian and author gave the name 'the Great Century' to the period of great missionary advance, 1800–1914.
15. Ruth Tucker, op. cit., p 109.
16. Elizabeth Goldsmith, *Roots and Wings* (Carlisle: OM, 1998) p 39. This delightful history of a missionary family for four generations was written by Royal Wilder's great-granddaughter.
17. The extent and speed of change is brilliantly described in *Future Shock* by Alvin Toffler (London: Pan Books, 1974).
18. Peter Brierley, Ed, *UK Christian Handbook* (UK, Evangelical Alliance/Bible Society/MARC, 1988).
19. Ralph D.Winter, 'The Kingdom Strikes Back: The Ten Epochs of Redemptive History', op. cit., p 140 (diagram adapted) in *Perspectives*.

20. Luke 9:2; 10:9; Matthew 10:1,8; Mark 6:12,13.
21. Ruth Tucker, op. cit., p 332.
22. Dorothy Clarke Wilson, *Ten Fingers for God* (London, Hodder & Stoughton, 1966). This book describes Paul Brand's missionary career and pioneer work in reconstructive surgery for leprosy patients.
23. Jackie Pullinger, *Crack in the Wall: Life and Death in Kowloon Walled City* (London: Hodder & Stoughton, 1973).
24. US Centre for World Evangelism, *Mission Frontiers Bulletin*, Jan. 2000.
25. John 4:35, 36 (The Living Bible).
26. Matthew 9:37 (The Living Bible).
27. Acts 16:6–10.
28. See James 5:14,15.
29. Matthew 8:19–22; Luke 9:57–62.
30. Mabel Williamson, *Have We No Right?* (London: China Inland Mission, 1958). This is a challenging and realistic book dealing with missionary sacrifices. For a brief review see Bibliography.
31. Larry Sharp, 'Towards a Greater Understanding of the Real MK: a review of recent research', *The Journal of Psychology and Christianity*, March 1986.
32. Jim Rymo, *Marching to a Different Drummer* (Washington: CLC, 1996) pp 49,50.
33. Michael Griffiths, *Tinker, Tailor, Missionary?* (Leicester: InterVarsity Press, 1992) p 132. An excellent review of the pros and cons of both long-term and short-term missionary work.
34. Thomas Hale, *On Being a Missionary* (Pasadena: William Carey Library, 1994).
    Bruce Nichols & Beulah Wood, Eds, *Sharing the Good News with the Poor* (Grand Rapids: Baker, 1996).
    Steve Hoke & Bill Taylor, *Send Me! Your Journey to the Nations* (Pasadena: William Carey Library, 1999).
    Daniel Bacon, *Equipping for Missions* (Littleton, CO: OMF, 1992).
35. Campbell Research, *Survey of Christian Baby-Boomers Regarding Missions as a Second Career* (Santa Maria, CA) pp 15, 23.
36. Acts 18:3; 20:34; 1 Corinthians 4:12; 2 Corinthians 11:7–12; 1 Thessalonians 2:9; 2 Thessalonians 3:8–10.
37. An excellent book for understanding Tentmaking, and preparing for it is: Jonathan Lewis (Ed) *Working Your Way to the Nations: A Guide to Effective Tentmaking* (Pasadena: William Carey Library, 1993).
38. Acts 1:8.
39. David and Margaret Bruce, Timaru, New Zealand.
40. A helpful book in how to share the gospel across cultures is *Only Connect* by David Claydon (Sydney: ANZEA, 1993).
41. Rev Dr David and Joyce Huggett are partners with Interserve. They have a retreat centre in Derbyshire known as The Oasis, and also run retreats for missionaries in many countries.
42. Some helpful books on supporting missionaries from the home base are:
    Serving as Senders by Neal Pirolo (Waynesboro: Operation Mobilisation, 1997).
    Re-Entry by Peter Jordan (Seattle: YWAM Publishing, 1992).
43. Adoniram Judson (1788–1850) pioneer missionary to Burma.
44. Emil Brunner (1889–1966) Swiss Christian theologian and author.

Conclusion

1. John 4:35.
2. Drs Sue and Brian Parry.
3. Ecclesiastes 9:10; 1 Corinthians 10:31.
4. Matthew 25:21.

A Selected Bibliography

The following books expand on some of the subjects mentioned in Celebrating Service. The order corresponds with the order these books are referred to in this book.

Freed to Serve by Michael Green (London: Hodder & Stoughton, 1983).
This book is written from the perspective of the ordained ministry within the Anglican Church. However, the author clearly defines New Testament guidelines for ministry in general and how these principles can be applied today.

Church: Why Bother? by Philip Yancey (Grand Rapids: Zondervan, 1998).
Yancey addresses the dilemma of the apparent irrelevance and inadequacies of the Church today. He reasons why Christians need to be a part of a church, based on his own journey of disillusionment, leaving the church and then returning to be a vital part of it.

Reaching Out by Henri Nouwen (London: HarperCollins, 1975).
In this challenging book Nouwen explores 'reaching out': to our innermost self; to our fellow human beings and to our God. He expands on ways of moving from hostility to hospitality.

The Wounded Healer by Henri Nouwen (London: Darton, Longman & Todd, 1994).
Nouwen maintains that we can only really serve out of our sense of woundedness. When our lives have been touched by the One who was wounded for us, we are able to become wounded healers ourselves.

Prayer: The Transforming Friendship by James Houston (Oxford: Lion, 1993).
Serving God becomes effective as we discover him through prayer. In learning to pray we enrich our service and become like the One we serve. This book is a superb aid for this journey.

God the Worker by Robert Banks (Sydney: Albatross, 1992).
The author explores the amazing way that God is portrayed throughout Scripture in a variety of metaphors depicting him as a worker and craftsman. These images are woven into the fabric of biblical teaching throughout the Old and New Testaments.

The New Pilgrims by John McInnes (Sydney, Albatross, 1980)
This book challenges us in a fresh way to gain a realistic but also a biblical perspective on important topics such as: time, simplicity, privacy, the place of the car in our society, work and leisure.

Slave of Christ by Murray Harris (Leicester: Apollos/IVP, 1999).
A scholarly yet reader-friendly study of the theme of slavery, looking at the historical context and biblical understanding of slavery. In the New Testament, being a slave (*doulos*) of Christ is frequently used and is a powerful metaphor for total devotion to him.

Serving One Another by Gene Getz (Wheaton: Victor, SP Publications, 1984).
This book is part of a study series designed to encourage renewal in the church. It covers a number of important and practical ways in which we can serve one another, particularly in the church.

Improving Your Serve by Charles Swindoll (London: Hodder & Stoughton, 1983).
This popular, easy-to-read portrait of the characteristics of true servants of Christ, shows how a servant should think and act. It includes a wide-ranging study of Scripture in relation to being a servant.

Celebration of Discipline by Richard Foster (London: Hodder & Stoughton, 1983).
A challenging book about a number of disciplines that are often neglected, such as meditation, fasting, simplicity, solitude and confession. Foster has an excellent chapter on the discipline of service, which he claims brings 'great liberty'.

Boundaries by Henry Cloud & John Townsend (Sydney: Strand, 1996).
The authors explain the importance of setting appropriate boundaries with your friends, spouse, children and at work. They provide many illustrations to show how boundaries apply in everyday living.

Network: The Right People in the Right Places for the Right Reasons by Bill Hybels and others (Grand Rapids: Zondervan, 1994).
The *Participant's Guide* is a workbook enabling you to identify your spiritual gifts, in order to help you serve effectively in the church. The programme is for individual or group use. *Implementation* and *Consultant Guides* are also available.

Devotional Classics by Richard Foster and James Smith (San Francisco: Harper, 1990).
This wonderful devotional aid introduces the writings of 52 'spiritual giants'. It covers the five main streams of Christian tradition referred to as Renovaré groups and each author features an introduction, excerpts from their writings and questions to explore further.

The Contemplative Pastor by Eugene Peterson (Grand Rapids: Erdmans, 1989).
A book full of rich ideas on how to lead a balanced life, 'passionate for God and compassionate with people'. The author writes freshly from his own experience as he challenges the reader concerning the work of the kingdom, personally and corporately.

Tinker, Tailor, Missionary? by Michael Griffiths (Leicester: IVP/OM Publishing, 1993).
This book is about the call, cost and direction of missionary service. It covers short- or long-term service, tentmaking or professional missionary work, church-planting or auxiliary ministries. Essential reading for anyone considering overseas service.

From Jerusalem to Irian Jaya by Ruth Tucker (Grand Rapids: Zondervan, 1983).
This book is a readable, informative and moving account of missionary endeavour over the past two millennia. The author does this mainly through brief biographies of over one hundred outstanding missionaries, bringing history to life.

Have We No Right? by Mabel Williamson (London: China Inland Mission, 1958).
This challenging little book, written by a missionary, looks at some of the 'rights' we usually take for granted and which are often lost on the missionfield. Can we assume such things as a normal living standard, health, privacy, romance, normal home life or even running things our own way are ours by right?

Marching to a Different Drummer by Jim Raymo (Fort Washington: CLC, 1996).
A stimulating, fresh look at cross-cultural missions today. The author challenges our culture's self-centred values which have influenced Christian thinking. He provides helpful discussion on the theology of mission and explores various aspects of missionary service.

Send Me! Your Journey to the Nations by Steve Hoke and Bill Taylor (Pasadena: William Carey Library, 1999).
An up-to-date guide to missionary training, divided into three sections: Getting Ready, Getting There and Getting Established. Full of practical and helpful information and ideas as well as work sheets to assess your progress.

Scripture References

GENESIS: 2:2; 8,9; 15; 3:21; 4:19–22;
12:3; 15:1, 6; ch.18

EXODUS: 3:12; 4:1–20; 9:1; 31:2–5, 17;
35:30–35

LEVITICUS: 19:18

DEUTERONOMY: 15:11

JOSHUA: 1:8

JOB: 10:8–9

PSALMS: 1:2; 8:3; 19:1; 23; 30:11; 41:9;
67:1–7; 80:1; 95:5; 82:3; 118:22–23;
119:19–20, 97, 99; 127:1–4

PROVERBS:11:18, 24, 25; 15:17; 19:17;
22:6; 25:21; 31:8–9

ECCLESIASTES: 9:10

ISAIAH: 28:16–17; 40:11; 42:1–4; 43:1–7;
45:9; 52:13–15; 53:1–11; 54:11–12;
58:10, 11; 61:10

JEREMIAH: 18:6; 31:10

EZEKIEL: 16:10; 31:8–9

JOEL: 2:28–29

MICAH: 2:12

ZECHARIAH: 13:7–9

MALACHI: 3:8–11

MATTHEW: 4:5–7, 18–19; 5:7–9, 12–14;
6:3; 8:19–22; 9:36, 37; 10:1, 8, 42; 11:29;
12:18–21, 38–39; 13:33; 14:14; 15:32;
18:1; 19–21, 24; 19:27–29; 20:1–16, 34;
22:37–40; 23:3, 8–12; 25:14–46;
26:20–25; 27:41–44

MARK: 1:16–17, 35–38, 41; 3:15, 21; 4:38;
6:12–13; 34, 46; 8:2; 9:33–37; 10:35–45;
12:1–11; 14:18–21

LUKE: 4:1, 14, 18–19; 6:38; 7:13, 22,
36–50; 8:48; 8:48; 9:2,46, 57–62; 10:9,
20, 21, 38; 11:1; 12:35–48; 14:1–6;
15:7,10; 17:10,19; 18:19; 22:21–27;
23:28–43; 24:21

JOHN: 1:14; 4:4–42; 5:17; 6:38; 7:5; 8:28,
34–35; 10:10,11; 12:1–4; 13:1–17, 21–30,
34–35; 14:6, 16; 15:1, 4–7, 8, 12, 15;
19:25–27; 21:1–23

ACTS: 1:2, 6, 8; 2:4, 18; 4:8, 27, 31; 6:1;
3–5; 7:55; 8:1–25; 9:17; 10:38; 11:19–21,
24, 27, 29; 13:1–4; 16:6–10; 17:31; 18:3;
20:19, 34; 24:17

ROMANS: 1:1; 4:3; 6:6, 16, 18, 22, 25–22;
7:14–25; 8:11, 26–27; 9:4, 20–21; 12:1–8;
14:10; 15:3, 16, 27

1 CORINTHIANS: 1:22; 3:6–17; 4:1–2, 5,
12; 5:5; 6:20; 7:23; 9:6, 19, 25–27; 10:24,
31; 12:1–11, 12–30; 16:1–4

2 CORINTHIANS: 1:3–4, 22; 4:5; 5:5, 10,
14; 6:1, 16; 8:2–15, 19–21; 9:6–11; 10:1;
11:7–12; 12:9–10

GALATIANS: 5:13, 14, 16, 22–23; 6:2–6

EPHESIANS: 1:13–14, 23; 2:16; 3:6, 20;
4:2, 4, 7–13, 16, 23, 28–29; 5:18, 21–33;
6:7, 18–19, 21

PHILIPPIANS: 1:1, 21; 2:3–8, 17, 25, 30

COLOSSIANS: 1:4, 7, 10, 12, 18, 20, 25;
2:19; 3:15, 22–24; 4:7, 12

1 THESSALONIANS: 2:9, 19–20; 4:11

2 THESSALONIANS: 3:7–10

1 TIMOTHY: 4:14; 5:8

2 TIMOTHY: 2:24; 3:17; 4:8

TITUS: 1:1; 3:1, 2

HEBREWS: 8:5; 9:1, 6, 14; 10:7,11: 6,
8–12, 13, 24, 39; 12:23; 13:2,15

JAMES: 1:1, 12; 2:8,14–18, 23; 4:6;
5:14–15

1 PETER: 1:18–19; 2:5, 9,16; 4:10; 5:2–6

2 PETER: 1:1; 2:17–19

1 JOHN: 2:1; 3:1–2; 4:7–8; 19, 20

JUDE: 1

REVELATION: 1:1; 2:10; 3:20; 12:10;
15:3; 20:11; 22:3–4, 12

216

Index

righteous, 29–30, 74, 148
Roman Empire, 129, 171–2
Romans, 79, 94, 102, 104
Rotary Club, 156
Russia, 171–2, 182

sacrifice(s), 34, 50, 69, 163, 192–3, 200
Saint, Nate, 187
Salvation Army, 179
Samaria, Samaritans, 157, 170
Satan, 79, 214
satisfaction, 39, 120–2, 127, 133, 138–9, 143
satisfying, 97, 121, 127, 140, 142, 189, 197, 201
Scandinavia, 173
Schweitzer, Albert, 181, 201
Scripture Union, 160
Scotland, 172, 208
Scudder, Ida, 181
Scudder, John, 181
secular, 32, 35, 67, 69, 139, 154, 158, 166, 175
self-centred, 90
self-esteem, 13–4, 75, 90, 93, 161
self-focus(ed), 19–20, 40
self-worth, 13, 23–4, 33, 75, 124
servant, 9, 11, 13–15, 23, 25, 27–9, 31–6, 39, 45, 47, 49, 51, 61, 68, 69, 71–4, 76–7, 79–6, 80–86, 90–3, 97, 102, 103, 105–7, 108, 109, 111–4, 118, 124, 126, 128–9, 131–2, 137, 146, 157, 167, 201–3
servant heart, 25, 31, 39, 92
servanthood, 28, 34, 44–5, 47, 61, 74–7, 85–6
Servant-king, 15, 71, 86, 157, 201
Servant leadership, 146, 158
Servant teacher, 74
Servants to the Asian Urban Poor, 187
serve, 10–13, 15–6, 19–21, 23–31, 34, 37, 39, 44, 52, 60, 62, 65, 67–8, 72, 74–6, 78–80, 84–6, 89–91, 102–6, 108–9, 112, 118, 124–5, 128, 131–2, 137, 139–41, 144, 146, 148, 150–2, 154, 156–8, 164, 167, 188–91, 200–3
service, 9–12, 13–14, 19–37, 39–61, 64–86, 114–134, 136–167, 169–200, 201–203.
service clubs, 156
service professions, 16, 137-8
sex, 20
shalom, 55, 57
Sider, Ronald, 154

SIM International, 178, 182
sin, 78-80, 201
singleness, 104, 140
slave(s), slavery, 9, 10, 14–5, 20, 26, 34–5, 45, 47, 54, 65, 72–5, 77–80, 86, 202
Slessor, Mary, 177
Smith, Adam, 149
Smith, Hannah, 35
social, social work, 14, 16, 46, 50, 53, 92, 110–11, 119–20, 123, 125, 140, 142–145, 149, 155, 160
socialisation, 19
social work, 14, 53, 110, 144–5, 160–1
Socrates, 65
solitude, 98, 107–8, 150, 220
Solomon, 21, 42, 46, 48
South America, 174, 197
Spanish, 174, 182
Specialised mission ministries, 180–188
spiritual, 20, 30–1, 50, 69–71, 92, 106–7, 111, 124, 126–8, 142–3, 152, 158, 160, 167, 194, 198–9, 202
spiritual direction, 110–111, 115
spiritual formation, 111, 194
spiritual gifts, 15, 102–5, 112–4, 158
sport, 20, 24, 152
stewardship, 68
storgë, 23
stranger, 29, 44
strong, 24, 26, 32, 42, 76, 107, 122, 126, 137, 142, 144, 147
Studd, C.T., 177
Student Christian Movement(SCM), 160
students, 42, 141–2, 145–6, 178, 187, 191, 197, 200
Student Volunteer Movement (SVM), 177
submission, 44–5, 47, 61
suffering, 28, 30, 51–3, 56–8, 71, 73–4, 104, 123, 139–40, 155-56, 189, 193, 203
Summer Institute of Linguistics (SIL), 184
sundouloi, 77
supervision, 110, 194
Swindoll, Charles, 84
sympathy, 9, 56, 58
synergy, 109

Tahiti, 176
talents, 68, 84, 93, 105, 107, 109, 131
Taylor, Hudson, 177, 180, 183
Taylor-Johnson Temperament Analysis (T-JTA), 100